Improve your spelling in English

Materials for learning
and teaching

Students' workbook

By Meryl Wilkins,
with a contribution by Pauline Moon

Published by NIACE

© 2012 National Institute of Adult Continuing Education
(England and Wales)

21 De Montfort Street

Leicester

LE1 7GE

Company registration no. 2603322

Charity registration no. 1002775

NIACE has a broad remit to promote lifelong learning opportunities for adults. NIACE works to develop increased participation in education and training, particularly for those who do not have easy access because of class, gender, age, race, language and culture, learning difficulties or disabilities, or insufficient financial resources.

You can find NIACE online at **www.niace.org.uk**

Cataloguing in Publications Data

A CIP record for this title is available from the British Library

ISBN 978-1-86201-554-8

Designed and typeset by Creative by Design, Oxfordshire, UK.
Printed and bound in the UK.

Contents

Introduction

This workbook, intended for use by adult ESOL learners working towards Entry Level 2 of the ESOL and Adult Literacy Curriculum (elementary level), can be used in either of the following ways:

- with a teacher in a class in which learners' writing is being developed (for example, adult ESOL or adult literacy). Teachers of these classes are referred to the teachers' guide of *Improve your spelling in English – Materials for learning and teaching*, which is available separately; or

- by learners working independently, at home, in class or in a learning centre. 'Notes for the learner' and 'Notes for the volunteer helper' sections are included within this Introduction.

The book

This material is intended primarily for adult ESOL (English for Speakers of Other Languages) learners who need to work on spelling in English. It can also be useful for other learners; i.e. people whose first language is English, if they need to work on spelling.

The level of the material is Entry 2 of the Adult ESOL Core Curriculum and the Adult Literacy Core Curriculum. The corresponding level for English language learners outside the UK would be 'elementary' or 'pre-intermediate'. However, some English language learners who have already reached a higher level in speaking, listening and reading, find that their writing is not at the same standard as their general use of English. They can also benefit from using this book.

Although this book can be used in class, it is designed to make self-study possible, as many learners will need to work on their spelling independently. Some of these learners may be attending ESOL or literacy classes or vocational courses, or taking a distance learning course. Others may be in employment or training, with a need or a wish to improve their writing. Provided they have an appropriate level of English, they should be able to use the book on their own. Those whose level of speaking, listening and reading is higher than their level in writing will probably be able to work entirely alone. Others will need occasional support from a teacher or the help of a volunteer. A volunteer helper may be anyone (friend, family member or someone who volunteered to give educational support), on condition that they are competent at spelling in English.

The following principles inform the way the book is organised:

- The importance of context – all spelling patterns are introduced in a context. Learners think about the meaning before they look at the spelling.

- Linking with real-life reading and writing – all the contexts are designed to be similar to familiar texts found in everyday life.

- Awareness of the fine line between the usefulness of recognising common patterns and the confusion of expecting more regularity in spelling than actually exists – in the book we look at 'patterns', not 'rules'. Learners are reminded in every unit that the pattern they have looked at may be common, but is not a hard and fast 'rule'.

- The use of a multi-sensory approach and the importance of developing strategies in line with preferred learning styles. There are many ways to learn spelling, and learners are encouraged to try different ones and think about what works best for them.

- The need to encourage individual learning and awareness of own progress – the book has a common format to make it easy to use, and there is an Answers section.
- The need to provide listening and sound discrimination practice where sound–symbol correlation is addressed – in all units, learners listen to the words being worked on. There are also sound discrimination exercises to help learners hear the difference between sounds (these can be carred out with the accompanying audio CD).

Units

Unit	Topic	Spelling pattern	Key words	Learn how to learn
1	Shopping lists	2 consonants, 1 sound – 'sh', 'ch', 'wh'	shirt, short, chicken, cheese, what, when	Consonants and vowels
2	Birthdays	2 consonants, 1 sound – 'th'	month, birthday, 5th, this, father	Pattern and rule
3	College	2 letters, 1 sound 1 letter, 2 sounds - 'c' & 'k'	college, key, centre, cinema, kitchen	Capital letters
4	Fitness	Short vowels	get, fit, fat, run, jog	Look, cover, write, check
5	Clothes	'ck' after short vowels	jacket, socks, black, pocket	How do you learn best?
6	Jobs	Common endings – 'er' & 'or'	waiter, doctor, actor, teacher, solicitor	Learn through seeing
7	Hotel work	Double consonants at end of words	staff, bill, jazz, bell, glass	Learn through hearing
8	Comparing people and places	Double consonants	bigger, hotter, wetter, slimmer, fatter	Learn through doing
9	Money	Vowels – silent 'e' with 'a'	save, take, make, safe, statement,	Letters and sounds
10	Bank accounts	Vowels – silent 'e' with 'o'	home, phone, code, close	Which words to learn?
11	Restaurants	Vowels – silent 'e' with 'i'	fine, white, rice, lime, pineapple	Split words into parts
12	Driving lessons	Dropping silent 'e'	driving, hoping, taking	Count the letters
13	In the town	Vowel sound 'ar'	market, car park, gardens	How important is correct spelling?
14	A holiday	'all'	ball, call, hall, waterfall, all	Read and notice
15	Supermarket shopping	Vowel sounds with 'ee' & 'ea'	Green beans, tea, cream, cheese,	Use a dictionary
16	The library	Vowel sounds with 'oo'	book, soon, room, cookery, look	Find spellings in a dictionary

Unit	Topic	Spelling pattern	Key words	Learn how to learn
17	The local council	Vowel sounds with 'ou' and 'ow'	round, down, town, outside	Work with a friend
18	Train travel	Vowel sounds with 'ai' and 'ay'	train, way, rail, pay, available	Work with the spell-check
19	Sightseeing	'igh'	high, right, try, fly, bright, sight, night	Be careful with a spell-check
20	Road signs	Vowel sounds with 'oa' and 'ow'	road, low, go, slow, boat show	Keep a personal spelling book
21	A personal account	Irregular plurals	babies, families, cities, companies	Learn common endings
22	A traditional story	'ed' endings	carried, tried, hurried, stopped, grabbed	Check your learning

Notes for the learner

The book

This material helps students with spelling in English.

There are 22 units. In each unit, there is a topic and a spelling pattern.

There are four pages in a unit. The layout is the same for each unit.

Page 1	Page 2
A text	Think about the spelling
Think about the meaning	– Find the words – Look and learn – Listen and learn
Read and notice	Be careful
Page 3	**Page 4**
Practise the spelling	Learn how to lear
Write	

Page 1

A text

This is a text to help you to notice spelling patterns. It is not a real-life text, but it looks similar to a real-life text.

Think about the meaning

Before you look at spelling patterns, make sure you understand what the text is about.

Read and notice

The text is not a real-life text, so look for similar texts in real life, read them and notice the spelling.

Page 2

Think about the spelling

When you understand the text, think about the spelling of the key words in the text

- Find the words
  Look at the text and find the words with the spelling pattern you are working on.

- Look and learn
  These activities help you learn the spelling pattern by using your eyes and hands.

- Listen and learn
  These activities help you learn the spelling pattern by listening. You will need to use the audio for this (see 'Using the CD', page 1).

You can do Look and learn first, or Listen and learn first. It is a good idea to choose which one you like to work with. For example, if you really don't like Listen and learn, don't do it! Do the activities that work best for you.

Be careful

English spelling is not regular, and you will find many words that do not fit the pattern. This section helps you to notice some common problems.

Page 3

Practise the spelling

On this page, there are exercises to practise the spelling pattern or to test yourself. The answers to these exercises are at the back of the book.

Write

Try to write something to practise the work of the unit. For this, you will need someone to check your work.

Page 4

Learn how to learn

Everybody has their own way of learning spelling. Read these pages and experiment to find ways that help <u>you</u>.

These pages on Learn how to learn are not connected to a topic or a spelling pattern. You can read them in any order you like. If you want, you can read them all before you start work on the spelling patterns.

Working independently

If you can read and understand the texts on page 1 of each unit without help, then you can probably work independently with this book. But it may be a good idea to find a volunteer helper. This can be any person such as a friend or family member. The person does not need to be a teacher, but they must be good at spelling in English.

If you are working independently, there are some things you need to know:

1. You need to read and understand the text on page 1 before you think about the spelling. It is important to understand the meaning of words before you think about the spelling. If you are not sure about the meaning, use a dictionary or ask somebody.

2. Different people learn in different ways. Read page 4 in Units 5, 6, 7 and 8 to find out more about this. Think about which way you learn best, and if there are activities you really don't like, don't do them. Do other activities instead.

3. You need to correct your own work. When you do an exercise, the Answers section will give you the answers, but before you look at the answers, check your work again to see if you have any mistakes.

4. If you find a mistake, write it out correctly. You can use the 'look, cover, write, check' method on page 4 of Unit 4.

5. At the end of page 3 in each unit, there is a section called Write. You will need to find someone to help you to mark this.

If someone is helping you, ask them to read the following section, 'Notes for the volunteer helper'.

Notes for the volunteer helper

If you have agreed to help a learner to use this material, you will need to read the 'Notes for the learner' above.

The main points to bear in mind as a volunteer helper are:

- The importance of the context
- Individual learning preferences
- Correcting and dealing with mistakes

The importance of the context

The learner should not be learning to spell any words he or she doesn't understand. Encourage the learner to read the text on page 1 of the unit for him/herself, then talk about the content of the text with you. If there are words that the learner doesn't understand, explain or demonstrate using pictures or mime.

If you speak the learner's first language, avoid translating for the learner. Discuss the text and the meaning of the words in English as much as you can. However, you can ask the learner to tell you the meaning of the words in their own language, as a check on understanding. If you don't speak the learner's language, you can ask him or her to check using a bilingual dictionary if they are unsure of the meaning of any key words.

Individual learning preferences

Different people learn in different ways, and some people have a very definite preference for the best way to learn. Before supporting a learner, you will find it useful to read all the Learn how to learn pages (page 4 of each unit), so that you can encourage him or her to try different approaches to learning and find which ways seem to work best for them.

On page 2 of each unit, there are different types of activity designed to help to learn spelling patterns. At first, it is a good idea to encourage the learner to use all of these approaches, but if it appears that the learner has particular difficulty with or an aversion to a particular method, do not ask him or her to persist. The important thing is to find an approach to learning which works for the learner.

Some learners will not want to do puzzles. Again, there is no point in doing these if there is no enjoyment in them. You can adapt these; for example, with a crossword, the learner can solve the clues but not bother with placing the answers in the grid.

Correcting and dealing with mistakes

Correcting exercises

As much as possible, the learner should be encouraged to find and correct his or her own mistakes. When the learner has completed one of the exercises (particularly those on page 3 of each unit), try to hold back from correcting immediately. Instead, ask the learner to take some time to check their own work. It is essential that learners get into the habit of proofreading what they have written.

They can also use the Answers section, instead of having the work corrected by you, as this will involve them looking more closely at what they have written.

If you do correct exercises, try not to give the correct spelling. Instead, indicate where the mistake is and ask the learner to think about how to correct it. When this procedure is established, you can move to a further stage in which you tell the learner only (for example) 'you have one mistake in this exercise'. The learner then has to find the mistake, and correct it.

When learners have made mistakes, it is important that they rewrite correctly the part they got wrong. They can do this using the 'look, cover, write, check' approach outlined in Unit 4, page 4. It is also important to revisit spelling patterns at a later date to see if the learner has remembered how to spell them.

Correcting the learner's writing

After completing the work of a unit, the learners are asked to do some free writing, relating to the topic of the unit and the text on page 1.

Before you correct this writing, make sure the learner has proofread it.

Also, before you correct, you will probably need to agree with the learner what you are correcting – the focus should be on the words involving the target spelling pattern and other key words connected with the topic. The focus should also be on spelling, rather than grammar and punctuation. If you try to correct everything, you risk demoralising the learner, which in turn can affect their confidence in their ability to learn. However, if the learner has few mistakes, it is more feasible to correct every one.

As with the correction of exercises, the learner should look at the misspelled words and write the correct version, using 'look, cover, write, check'. However, if there are a lot of spelling mistakes, you will need to select which ones to work on. To get an idea of how to select words to work on, read page 4 of Unit 10.

If the learner has written a long text with lots of mistakes, it is a good idea to encourage him or her to write less, but to take more time over the writing.

Reading the learner's writing can also give you an idea of where their mistakes are, and which spelling patterns, or which individual words, they need to work on next.

Using the CD

Included with this workbook is an audio CD which contains spoken examples of the text provided in the exercises for all 22 units. The tracks on the CD you'll need to listen to are listed in a box at the beginning of each unit in the text, recognised by this icon

As you work through the exercises in each unit, you will also then see a headphones icon and an audio clip number, which will guide you to the relevant audio clip for that exercise: **1.1**

The audio clip number will be spoken before each example on the CD.

UNIT 1
Shopping lists

Consonants – two letters make one sound, 'sh', 'ch', and 'wh'

 Please refer to tracks 2–8 on the audio CD for this unit.

Sara is going shopping. She needs to buy clothes for her son as well as food.

Dear Parent

As you may know, we have our school sports day next Friday, the 17th of April.

Your child needs to bring:
A pair of shorts
A T-shirt (with short sleeves)
A pair of trainers or running shoes

If you wish to come to the sports day, you will be welcome. We start at 1.30 p.m.

Yours sincerely

J. Ahmed (head teacher)

Shopping list
Chicken legs
Fish
Tea bags
Milk
Cheddar cheese
Butter
Bread
Ice cream
Chocolate sauce

Think about the meaning

1 Who sent the letter from the school?
Why does Sara need to buy clothes for her son?
When is the school sports day?

2 Where do you go to buy clothes?
Which shop do you go to for food?

Read and notice

Read letters and notes from schools.
Look on the Internet for sites that sell clothes and food.

Think about the spelling

1 **Find the words**

Take three different colours and highlight all the words on the facing page beginning with 'sh', 'ch', 'wh'. Look at the letter, the shopping list and the questions.

2 **Look and learn**

a) 'sh' and 'ch'

Find 'sh' words on the facing page and write them on one piece of paper. Do the same with 'ch' words. Like this:

b) 'wh' question words: when, where, who, why, what

Find or draw a picture for each word. Write the word with 'wh' in black and the other letters in another colour.

When   Where   Who   Why   What

3 **Listen and learn**

Listen to 'wh' words, then say aloud the letters in the words

a) Who w – h – o   what w – h – a – t   where w – h – e – r – e.   **1.1**

b) Listen to words with 'sh' and 'ch' and notice the difference.   **1.2**

c) Look at the pictures, read the words and listen.   **1.3**

1 Ships   2 Chips

When you hear a word, put your finger on the right picture.

Listen again, and write the words in the order you hear them.

Be careful

Some words don't follow the pattern, e.g.

'sugar' has the 'sh' sound, but only an 's',

'ch' can sound like 'k'; e.g. 'chemist',

'school' has 's', 'c', and 'h', but the pronunciation is like 'sc' or 'sk'.

Practise the spelling

1 Read these words and write them on separate pieces of paper: words with 'sh' on one and words with 'ch' on the other (sometimes 'sh' is at the beginning, sometimes at the end).

children	ship	fish and chips	change	she	chest	chair	shop
shoes	shoulder	shy	cheap	champion	English		

2 Read these sentences, then write 'sh' or 'ch' in each space. You can do it with or without the audio.

 1.4

a) Engli sh... people love fi..sh. and ......ips.

b) My ......ildren need new ......oes.

c) The big ......ops are expensive, but the market is ......eap.

d) We bought a table and four new ......airs.

e) Her daughter doesn't speak much. ..sh..e's a very ..sh..y girl.

f) Can you ......ange a £20 note?

g) I had an accident and hurt my ..sh..oulder and my ..ch..est.

h) Who will win the football ......ampion......ip this year?

3 Write the correct question word in each space.

a) .When....... did you arrive here?   Yesterday.

b) ..Who....... is your teacher?   Mr. Green.

c) ..What....... do you want?   A bit of help.

d) .Where....... do you live?   In Manchester.

e) .How....... many children have you got?   Three, two girls and a boy.

f) .Why....... do you want this job?   I am interested in working in the tourist industry.

4 Listen again to Audio 1.2 and write the words you hear.

 1.2

Write

Write a list of food you want to buy.
Write a list of clothes you need for work or for school.

Learn how to learn

Consonants and vowels

1   The alphabet

Read the alphabet. Check that you know the order of the letters, then write the alphabet without looking.

a   b   c   d   e   f   g   h   i   j   k   l   m   n   o   p   q   r   s   t   u   v   w   x   y   z

Read the alphabet again and say the names of the letters aloud.   **1.5**

Be especially careful with: a, e, i, g, j, k, c, s, q, r, y.

Listen to the audio and check that you got the names right.

All letters of the alphabet are either consonants or vowels. There are 21 consonant letters and five vowel letters ('y' is a consonant, but it often does the work of a vowel).

Take two pens in different colours. On the alphabet above, circle the 21 consonants in one colour and the five vowels in another colour.

2   Consonants

There are 21 consonant letters, but there are 24 consonant sounds

Listen to the audio and notice the consonant sounds.   **1.6**

B bag	G gentle	L lamp	R road	X box	Th this
C cup	G going	M man	S sun	Y yellow	Th thing
C cinema	H hat	N nose	T table	Z zoo	Wh what
D dance	J jam	P party	V village	Sh shoe	Ng sing
F fish	K kitchen	Q quick	W wall	Ch chair	

There are 24 sounds altogether.

Look at 'cup' and 'kitchen'. They have the same sound, but different letters. Find two other words with the same sound, but two different letters.

Look at 'cinema' and 'cup'. They have the same letter, but two different sounds. Find two other words with the same letter, but two different sounds.

Find words where two letters together make one sound.

3   Vowels

There are only five vowel letters (+ 'y', which can do the work of a vowel), but there are 19 vowel sounds.

Listen to the audio and you will hear 19 words. Each word has a different vowel sound.   **1.7**

again	hand	road	car	right
see	bus	soon	rain	boy
big	hot	put	near	now
leg	law	girl	where	

In the units of this book, we can see some of the ways to write these many different vowel sounds.

Consonants – two letters make one sound, 'th'

 Please refer to tracks 9–10 on the audio CD for this unit.

Read the email from Krystyna to her friend Nuria.

| Send | Attach | Insert | Priority | Signature |

To: Nuria
Cc:
Subject:
Attachments: *none*

10 · B *I* U T

Hi Nuria

How are you? Hope you and the family are all well.

I am writing to invite you to a party on the 19th – it's a Saturday. It's a birthday party, but not just for one person – there are three of us with birthdays this month. My birthday was on the 4th, my son Adam has a birthday on the 17th, the Thursday before the party, then my daughter Teresa will be thirteen on the 27th. We had separate parties before, but decided to do it differently this year, because the children are getting older.

So I hope you can come, and bring your family, of course, any time from 6pm. By the way, I think you met my father last year – he is coming. My brother and sister-in-law are coming too, with their children. Did you meet them when you were here before? I can't remember.

Let me know if you can come. I hope so.

Krystyna

Think about the meaning

1 Look at the calendar.
   Mark the birthdays of Krystyna and her children and the date of the party.

Monday	Tuesday	Wednesday	Thursday	Friday	Saturday	Sunday
	1	2	3	Krysta 4	5	6
7	8	9	10	11	12	13
14	15	16	Adam 17	18	Party 19	20
21	22	23	24	25	26 Te..	27
28	29	30	31			

2 If the month in the calendar is October, write some of the dates out in full, e.g.
   Monday, the 14th of October.
   Thursday, the 24th of October.

Read and notice

Read emails and other sorts of invitations.
Read dates on calendars and letters. Are they all written the same way?

Think about the spelling

1 Find the words

Look in the text on the facing page and underline all the words with 'th'. Sometimes 'th' is at the beginning of the word, sometimes in the middle, and sometimes at the end.

2 Look and learn

a) Some very common words begin with 'th', eg. the, there, this, that, then, these, those.
Read these words and think about the meaning:

This is my book

That is your book

There is a book on the table

These are my books

Those are your books

b) Use this method to learn to spell common words:

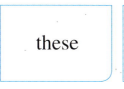

1 Look at the word   2 Cover it   3 Write it   4 Check

3 Listen and learn

a) Listen to the following words:

this; that; these; those; there   🎧 **2.1**

b) There are two different 'th' sounds, but they are very similar.
Look at the two lists of words and listen.   🎧 **2.2**

Sound 1	**Sound 2**
three	this
birthday	brother
month	father
think	then

Can you hear the two different sounds?

Be careful

There are two words which sound exactly the same, but have different spelling:

There is a lot to do.

They are coming with *their* children.

In a few words 'th' sounds like 't', e.g. in the name 'Thomas'.

Practise the spelling

1 Practise 'th'.

Lots of common words begin with 'th'.

Nuria is showing her family photos to her friends at work. One of the photos is of her son's wedding. Read what she says and choose the right word to put in each gap.

This / These   ……… is a picture of my son's wedding.

Than / That   …………… young woman is my daughter.

This / These   …………people are my relatives.

That / Those   ………… people are friends.

My son had a big wedding.

There / These   ……… were about 50 people.

then / the   at ………… ceremony.

they / than   and more ………… 200 at the party.

2 Practise common endings with 'th'.

'ther' is a common ending for words: add 'ther' to the word beginnings.

bro .ther..   ano .ther..   fa .ther..

mo .ther..   wea .ther..   toge .ther..

Then put the words in the gaps:

a) My …brother….. and …………………… live in India.

b) If the …weather….. is nice, we can sit in the park.

c) Would you like …another………… cup of tea?

d) If you want to go swimming, we can go …………………

e) I have two sisters and one …brother…………..

3 Listen again to Audio 2.2 and write the words you hear.   **2.2**

Write

Write about your family and their birthdays.
Write an email to a friend, inviting him or her to a party.

Learn how to learn

Pattern and rule

Do you already read and write in another language?

If you do, is that language regular in its spelling?

In many languages one letter represents one sound, and is always the same. English is not regular, so it is difficult to learn rules.

In this book, we look at 'patterns', not 'rules'.

What is the difference between rules and patterns?

A rule is always true, or nearly always true. English has some spelling rules, but not many.

A pattern means that a lot of words have a similar spelling. A pattern is often true, but not always true. It may be true 50%, 70%, 90% of the time. Even when there are a lot of words with the same sound and pattern, you will probably find other words that do not fit the pattern.

For example:

'cheese', 'chair', 'children' all have the same spelling pattern ('ch') and the same sound, but 'chemist' has the same spelling but a different sound.

'red', 'leg' and 'bed' all have the same spelling pattern and sound, but 'bread' has the same sound with a different spelling.

It is very difficult to learn English spelling by rules, but you can learn by looking at patterns, as long as you know it does not work all the time. However, if you can already spell in another language, you may find you cannot learn in the same way as you learned that language. You may need to find new ways of learning to spell in English.

In this book, we look at patterns, not rules. It can be very useful to look at words with a similar spelling pattern, but you cannot expect all words with the same sound to fit that pattern.

And remember:

If you find English spelling difficult, you are not alone.

English spelling is difficult for lots of people, even if they went to school in Britain and have good qualifications. Some teachers have problems with spelling!

UNIT 3
College

c and k – two letters, one sound; one letter, two sounds

 Please refer to tracks 11–12 on the audio CD for this unit.

Look at the website for Westwood Catering College.

WESTWOOD CATERING COLLEGE

About us   Course information   Job vacancies   Contact us   Find us

Find us

Westwood Catering College is situated one mile north of the city centre.

Take bus 301 or 76 from King Street bus station.

The 301 stops outside the college.

If you catch the 76, get off outside the Odeon Cinema, turn left and left again, and cross the road to the college.

Maps – Finding the college

Map of the college campus

| Library | Computer centre | | Key Skills department | Student common room |

| | Staff canteen | | Student canteen | |

| Kitchens 6–10 | | | Kitchens 1–5 |

Upstairs to classrooms 11–19

CAR PARK

About us   Course information   Job vacancies   Contact us   Find us   Site map

Think about the meaning

1 What do people learn in a catering college?

key skill

2 Are the sentences true or false?

The college is south of the city centre. T	True / False
The 301 bus stops outside the college.	True / False
The buses go from Queen Street bus station.	True / False
There are separate canteens for students and staff.	True / False
The Library is next to the Key Skills department.	True / False
Classrooms 11–19 are upstairs.	True / False

Read and notice

Read maps and directions, on the Internet and on paper.
If you go to college, find and read a map of the college.
Look at websites of different colleges.

Think about the spelling

1 Find the words

Find and underline these words on the website on the facing page:

college; campus; catering; catch; city; cinema; cross; centre; canteen; king; key; kitchens; classrooms; computer; common; car; course; contact.

2 Look and learn

a) Write the five vowel letters on a piece of paper. Read the words below and look at the second letter. Write the words on the paper under the right vowel letter. Circle the first two letters.

canteen   key   college   computer   kitchens   catering

king   car   cup   keyboard   kettle   coffee

What is the second letter?

a	e	i	o	u
canteen	key			

b) **Notice:** When do you use 'k' and when do you use 'c'? (Look at the second letter to help you decide.)

3 Listen and learn   **3.1**

a) Look again at the words in **1** and **2** and listen at the same time.
Notice the sound at the beginning of each word.
Write each word in the correct column.

Begins with 'k'	Begins with 'c' 'c' sounds like 'k' in 'king'	Begins with 'c' 'c' sounds like 's' in 'sing'	Begins with 'c' Another consonant follows
King	college	city	cross
Which two vowels can follow 'k'?	Which three vowels can follow 'c'?	Which two vowels can follow 'c'?	

b) **Notice**

When does 'c' sound like 'k' in 'king'?
When does 'c' sound like 's' in 'sing'?

Be careful

Some words sound the same but have a different spelling: e.g. centre ('c') but 'sent' ('s').

Practise the spelling

1 Look again at the map on page 10 and answer the questions:

Where can you find cars?   In the ....

Where can you find a kettle?   In the ....

Where can you find a keyboard?   In the ....

Where can you find cups of coffee?   In the ....

2 Write 'c' or 'k' in the gaps:

Would you like a ...up of ...offee?

I lost my ...ey and had to ...all my husband at work.

... an you help me in the ...itchen?

I need to buy a new ...eyboard for my ...omputer.

... an I help you? Thank you, that's very ...ind of you.

Our ... at had six ...ittens.

If you can't spell the words, look at the second letter. What normally comes before it – 'c' or 'k'?

3 Look at another consonant with two sounds.

'g' can have a hard sound, or a soft sound like 'j'.

Read these sentences and decide if the 'g' has a hard or soft sound:

> Ladies and Gentlemen.
> Get off the bus at the bus station.
> Can you give me a hand?
> Their house has a lovely garden.
> He speaks French and German.
> She's secretary to the General Manager.

Listen to Audio 3.2 and check your answers.   🎧 **3.2**

But notice: using 'g' does not follow a regular pattern. For example, 'ge' may have a hard sound or a soft sound.

4 Look at other consonants. Play a word game.

Take a consonant and think of: a country; a city; a food; something in the house.

Example: Bangladesh; Birmingham; bananas; bed.

Do the same with d; f; l; m; n; p; r; s; t

Write

1 Choose four or five words beginning with 'c' or 'k', and write four or five sentences (one for each word).

2 Draw a map of a building you know well, and label it.

Learn how to learn

Capital letters

1 When we write in English, we use a capital letter for the first letter of the first word in a sentence. There are also some words which have a capital letter even when they are not the first word in a sentence.

Find some of these on the first page of this unit (page 10) and the first page of Unit 2 (page 6).

When you write the days of the week or the months, you start with a capital letter, e.g. Thursday, October

Write lists of the seven days of the week, and the 12 months of the year.

2 When you write the name of a person or a place, you start with a capital letter, e.g.

Names of people	John Brown; Usha Patel
Names of places	New York; Tehran; Egypt; South America
Names of streets	High Street; Leeds Road
Names of rivers	River Nile
Names of mountains	Mount Everest
Names of buildings	the Empire State Building
Names of shops	Marks and Spencer

3 Write the names of people, places, streets, rivers, mountains and shops that you know.

Look at the examples:

a) We crossed the River Thames. b) I walked along Manchester Road.
a) We crossed the river.   b) I walked along the road.

Look at the words 'river' and 'road'.

Why is there a capital letter in the first and not the second?

4 Cross out the wrong word, e.g.

a) The President of the United States lives in the White House / house.

b) My uncle has a nice House / house.

c) I live in a noisy street / Street.

d) My address is 40 High street / Street.

e) Cairo is a city on the river / River Nile.

f) I like to walk by the river / River in the evening.

g) This is a very old building / Building.

5 Change letters to capitals where necessary:

I like london. I have a flat near hammersmith bridge. When I want to go anywhere, I get the train from hammersmith station. I like to go to oxford street, as there are some good shops there, for example selfridges. I often go there on a saturday. Sometimes, I like to walk in hyde park. There is a park near my home, but it's quite small.

Fitness

Short vowels

 Please refer to tracks 13–16 on the audio CD for this unit.

Read what these friends wrote on a social network site.

Matt:	I am totally unfit! I need to get fit before I start my new job. Help! How do I do it? Any ideas?
Comment – Anna:	Do what I do. I swim three times a week.
Comment – Tom:	Do ten push-ups every morning – that works!
Comment – Abdul:	Do the same as me – go for a run in the park every Sunday.
Comment – Lam:	I jog in the park every morning – come with me next time.
Comment – Ben:	Play golf – it's exercise and it's fun.
Comment – Sam:	Don't be lazy. Don't get the bus to work – walk! If not the whole way, walk to the next bus stop.
Comment – Shiv:	I put lots of weight on last year, but I'm OK now. Eat low-fat food, and if you get hungry between meals, don't eat, drink some water instead.

Think about the meaning

1 Who thinks it's good to eat low fat food?

2 Who thinks golf is fun?

3 Who jogs in the park every morning?

4 Who swims three times a week?

5 Who thinks push-ups can help?

6 Who thinks it's a good idea to walk to the next bus stop?

7 Who runs in the park every Sunday?

8 Which of the things above do you do?

Read and notice

Read magazine articles and leaflets about health, exercise and diet.
Look for websites about fitness and exercise.
Read messages on social networking sites.

Think about the spelling

1 Find the words

Find and underline these words in the text on the facing page.

fat   get   fit   up   jog   swim   ten   push   bus   drink   lots
stop   run   golf   job   help   fun   put

2 Look and learn

Write the words above in the table below, according to the vowel letter. Add these words to the table: back, hand, leg, left, neck and hip.

a	e	i	o	u
fat	get			

Notice: How many vowel letters are there in each word?

How many consonant letters are there at the end of the word?

3 Listen and learn

a) Listen to the words in Audio 4.1.   **4.1**

All the words have a short vowel sound.

There are only five vowel letters, but there are six short vowel sounds. We write 'u' for two different sounds. Notice the difference between the sound in 'fun' and 'bus' and the sound in 'put' and 'push'.

b) Hear the difference between the short vowel sounds.   **4.2**

Look at the pictures, read the words and listen.

Pin   Pen   Cap   Cup
Man   Men   Pot   Put

Listen to the same words in a different order.   **4.3**

When you hear a word, put your finger on the right picture.

Listen again, and write the words in the order you hear them.

Be careful

Short vowel sounds do not always have the same spelling as in the examples here. Same pronunciation – different spelling:

son – my son and my daughter

sun – the sun is shining

Practise the spelling

1   Say the names of the things in the pictures.

Put the right vowel letter in the gap. There is only one letter for each gap.

The vowel sounds in these words are short vowel sounds, and you can hear them on the audio. If you like, you can listen to the audio as you write, or you can write first and listen to Audio 4.4 afterwards.

 4.4

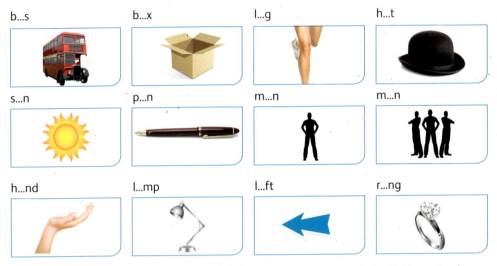

b...s   b...x   l...g   h...t

s...n   p...n   m...n   m...n

h...nd   l...mp   l...ft   r...ng

There are many more vowel sounds in English, but it is a good idea to start with these simple ones.

2   Play a word game with consonants and vowels.

Look at the word chain. Only one letter changes each time.

big – bag – bad – bed

Try to make word chains, starting with: ten; pen; sit; man; put

Look at this word chain. The chain comes back to the first word.
Can you make a chain like this?

big – bag – bad – bed – bet – let – leg – beg – big

3   Listen again to Audio 4.1 and write the words you hear.

 4.1

Write

Write your own ideas about what to do to get fit.

Write a message on a social network site

Learn how to learn

Look, cover, write, check

There are different ways to remember spellings, and we give ideas about these in every unit of this book.

One very useful method is the 'look, cover, write, check' method, especially for words which do not follow a common pattern, such as these words:

friend
school
because

How to do 'look, cover, write, check'

1 First, take an exercise book or a blank page in a file, and divide it into four columns.

2 Write the words you want to learn in column 1. Ask someone to check that the spelling is correct.

3 Think about which part of the word will be difficult to remember, e.g. 'ie' in 'friend', 'sch' in 'school', 'au' in 'because', and find a way to help you remember this part of the word (e.g. write it bigger, underline it, or highlight it, or say it aloud to yourself).

1	2	3	4
fr ie nd			
sch ool			
because			

4 Look at the word, say it aloud, close your eyes and try to 'see' it in your head.

5 Take a piece of thick paper and cover the word.

6 Without looking at column 1, write the word in column 2.

7 Say it as you write it, and think about the part that you expected to be difficult to remember.

8 Look again at column 1, and check the spelling of the word you wrote in column 2, letter by letter.

9 If you made a mistake, write it again.

10 The next day, do the same again, with column 3.

11 *2 or 3 days later*, do the same again, with column 4.

12 About a week later, test yourself, or ask someone else to test you.

Think about when and where you will work on spelling.

- After dinner?
- When the children are in school?
- When you first come home from work?

Clothes

'ck' after short vowels

 Please refer to tracks 17–20 on the audio CD for this unit.

Read these advertisements for cheap clothes, advertised in a magazine.

MEN'S AND LADIES' JEANS

ONLY £14.99 A PAIR

Pockets front
and back
Blue or black

Small, medium,
large

THICK WINTER SOCKS

BLACK OR WHITE

One size fits all

£7.99 per pack
of six pairs

LADIES' DENIM JACKETS

Button front

Two front pockets

Sizes 10–16

£24.99 each

SPECIAL OFFER – *order now, and get*
*postage and packing **ABSOLUTELY FREE!***

Think about the meaning

1 What are the colours available for jeans?

2 Where are the pockets on the jeans?

3 Are the socks for hot or cold weather?

4 How many pairs of socks can you get for £7.99?

5 What size of jackets can you buy?

6 How much do you pay for postage and packing if you order now?

Read and notice

Read adverts for clothes in newspapers and magazines.

Look for websites which sell clothes.

Think about the spelling

1 Find the words

Look at the advertisements again and underline all the words with 'ck' in the middle or at the end. There are eight different words.

2 Look and learn

Here are eight more words (check that you understand the meaning): clock; chicken; lucky; check; sick; neck; truck; quickly

Look at all 16 words, and put them in vowel letter groups. 'a' is started for you:

a			e			i			o			u	
bl	ack												
j	ack	et											

| vowel+ck | This can help you remember the pattern.

3 Listen and learn

i) 'ck' normally comes after short vowel sounds. Listen to the 16 words from **1** and **2**, and notice the vowel sound that comes before 'ck'.   **5.1**

ii) Notice the difference between short vowel sounds.   **5.2**

Listen to the pairs of sentences.

a) My favourite song is on this CD, on **track** 3.

b) My brother drives a **truck** taking food to supermarkets.

c) Can you **lock** the door before you go?

d) Good **luck** with your exam.

e) A **chick** is a baby chicken.

f) Can you **check** my work for me, please?

iii) Listen to the single words and say which sentence they come from (a, b, c, d, e or f).   **5.3**

Be careful

1 Normally, there is only one vowel letter before 'ck'. The word 'quickly' has two vowels before 'ck'. But the 'u' is not part of the vowel sound. It belongs with the 'q'. A 'u' always comes after a 'q'.

2. Not all words with the same consonant sound at the end use 'ck'. It is only words with a short vowel sound. Words with the same vowel letter but a different vowel sound will have a different ending, e.g 'take', 'cake', 'like'.

Practise the spelling

1 Read the sentences below, think about the meaning of the words and put the right word in the gap.

a) Can you .... the door when you leave? (luck / lock)

b) Good .... with your exam. (luck / lock)

c) My brother drives a .... (truck / track)

d) This is my favourite .... on this CD. (truck / track)

e) I bought a .... of biscuits. (packet/pocket)

f) There's a hole in my coat .... (packet/pocket)

g) What time is it? 6 o' .... (click / clock)

h) To reach the website, ... on the link. (click / clock)

2 Listen to the audio and fill the gaps in the story below.   🎧 **5.4**

N .... was a .... driver. He had to travel from England to France and .... three times a week and he sometimes got very tired.

This morning he had to get up at 5 o' .... to start work. The alarm went off and he woke, but went .... to sleep, then woke up again suddenly at 5.30.

He jumped out of bed and ran downstairs. He grabbed his .... but a .... of cigarettes fell out of the .... When he bent down to .... it up, he moved too .... and hurt his .... and his .... so badly that he felt ....

In the end, he just went .... to bed and forgot about work until the next day.

Write

1 Choose four or five words with 'ck' in the middle or at the end, and write four or five sentences (one for each word).

2 Look in catalogues and magazines that sell mail-order clothes.

Look also in online catalogues.

Practise filling in the order forms.

Learn how to learn

How do you learn best?

Some very common words do not follow a pattern, e.g.

friend   people   beautiful

You need to find ways to remember them.

There are many different ways to remember spellings.

Find the way that is best for you personally.

Your eyes can help you remember

If you see a word again and again, it can help you to remember it.

Reading can help with spelling.

Your ears can help you remember

If you say the spelling of a word aloud, it can help you to remember it.

Your hand can help you remember

When you write a word correctly, it can help you to remember the spelling.

Different people learn in different ways

Some people like to use their eyes a lot, some like to use their ears and others like to use their hands. Many people use all three ways of remembering.

Take some words you are trying to learn at the moment, and try different ways of remembering them.
- Look at the words again and again.
- Say the words and the spelling aloud.
- Write the words.

What works best for you?
- Eyes?
- Ears?
- Hand?
- A combination of all of them?

You can work with a computer

Which do you prefer?
- Working with pen and paper.
- Working with a computer.
- Both.

In this book, there are different ideas for learning and remembering spelling. Try them, and use the ideas that work best for you.

UNIT 6
Jobs

Common endings 'er' and 'or'

 Please refer to tracks 21–22 on the audio CD for this unit.

Read about three people's work.

Yusuf's story

In my country, I was a taxi driver, but now I am a waiter in a Turkish restaurant. I have three children, all at school. My daughter wants to be a teacher, and my older son wants to be a lawyer. My other son says he wants to be an actor or a singer, but I don't like that idea.

Anna's story

I have a part-time job as a cleaner, but I don't like it. It's hard work and I don't meet many people.

I want to start college in September, because I would like to have a different job in the future. I would like to be a hairdresser.

Samira's story

I speak Arabic, but I'm learning English, because I need it in my daily life. A lot of people at my work speak Arabic, but the manager and the supervisor speak only English.

When I go to the doctor or to my solicitor, my friend comes with me to help with English, but I want to be independent and do things for myself.

Think about the meaning

Say whether the sentences are true or false.

a) Yusuf is a taxi driver now   True / false

b) Yusuf's daughter wants to be a teacher   True / false

c) Yusuf's older son wants to be an actor   True / false

d) Anna works full-time as a cleaner   True / false

e) Anna likes her job   True / false

f) Anna would like to be a hairdresser   True / false

g) Samira's manager speaks Arabic   True / false

h) Samira has a solicitor   True / false

i) Samira wants to be independent   True / false

Read and notice

Read people's life stories in student magazines and books.

Think about the spelling

1 Find the words

Find and underline all the words for jobs on the facing page.

2 Look and learn

a) You will need three pens: black and two other colours.

b) Write the words for jobs in the table: write the main part of the word in black, then write 'er' in one colour and 'or' in another.

Words ending in '**er**'	Words ending in '**or**'
wait**er**	doct**or**

c) Add the right ending to these words. Use a dictionary if you don't know the spelling.

doct....	driv....	act....	clean....
solicit....	wait....	danc....	football....

d) There are three words in the text on the facing page that end in 'er' but are not jobs. What are the three words?

e) Look at all the words in the text again and decide which ones are important for you personally to learn. For example, if you have a daughter, the word 'daughter' is important. If you are a waiter, the word 'waiter' is important. Decide which part of the word is difficult to remember; for example, 'augh' in 'daughter'. Write these letters extra large or in a different colour to help you remember them.

da ugh ter   w ai ter

3 Listen and learn

Listen to the words. Notice that the vowel sound at the end of the words is the same for words ending in 'er' and words ending in 'or'.   🎧 **6.1**

Be careful

1 Sometimes there are different spelling patterns in different countries. For example, in Britain, people write 'go to the theatre' and 'the centre of town'. In America, they write 'theater' and 'center'.

2 Some words have the same vowel sound at the end but a different spelling; e.g. 'future'.

Practise the spelling

1 Listen to the audio and fill the gaps in these sentences. **6.2**

My son wants to be a ....

My .... is a ....

My .... and .... are ....

.... earn lots of money

I worked as a .... before I came to the UK.

2 The exercise below is for students who are in a class with a teacher.

Each student takes a card with a picture of a job. Don't *read* the name of the job. Walk around the room and talk to other students. Does the name of the job on your card end in 'er' or 'or'? Make two groups of students, one group with 'er' words and one group with 'or' words. Which group is bigger?

3 Find the word that fits the meaning and write it in the grid below. All the words have 'er' or 'or' at the end. When you have finished, an extra word appears down the middle.

1) Not a brother, a ....

2) This person works in the theatre.

3) This person works in offices, homes, schools, everywhere.

4) This person works in a restaurant.

5) This person works with sick people.

6) There is one of these on every bus.

7) A male parent.

8) A sportsman, member of a team.

9) This person cuts hair.

	1 S	I	S	T	E	R				
2										
	3									
	4									
	5									
	6									
	7									
	8									
9										

Listen again to Audio 6.1 and write the words you hear. **6.1**

Write

Write about your job or the job you would like. Write about the people you know and the jobs they do or would like to do.

Learn how to learn

Learn by seeing

Do you remember things well if you see them?

You can try different ways to remember spellings.

- Write the word larger than normal and look at it again and again.

people

- Write the words you want to learn on large card and stick them to the wall or on the door where you live. You will see them again and again, even when you are not thinking about spelling.

- Use colour. You can write the consonants in one colour and the vowels in another colour.

P e o p l e

- You can write words with the same pattern in the same colour. For example, write the word 'green' with a green pen.

green

Then write other words with the same spelling pattern in green pen too.

sleep; teeth; street; feet

- Think about the part of the word that is difficult to remember (e.g. 'eo' in 'people'). Write this part in a different colour from the rest of the word.

P e o p l e

- Write the part that is difficult to remember separately from the rest of the word.

p / eo / ple

- Use a computer to write the word a few times (make sure it is correct), then put each one into a different font. Look at them all and decide which one you like, e.g.

people

people

people

people

- Close your eyes and try to 'see' the word in your head, maybe in big, gold letters.

Hotel work

Double consonants at end of words

 Please refer to tracks 23–24 on the audio CD for this unit.

Read the texts connected with hotels.

a)
WHITE HORSE INN

VACANCIES

BAR STAFF required for Friday and Saturday evening
WAITER or WAITRESS to work full time in new grill room

b)
DRINKS MENU

House red wine	bottle	£14.50
	glass	£4.50
House white wine	bottle	£14.00
	glass	£4.00
Mineral water	sparkling	£3.50
	still	£3.00

c)
Application for Employment

Name   Address

d)
MUSIC NIGHT
Live jazz band every Sunday
Don't miss it

e)
For groups of more than ten people, we add 10% service charge to the bill

f)
DO NOT PUT GLASS IN THIS DISHWASHER

Think about the meaning

1 Where can you expect to see the texts?

In a newspaper, on a form, in a kitchen, on the menu, outside the restaurant?

a) ....

b) ....

c) ....

d) ....

e) ....

f) ....

2 Write a word that means:

a) People who work in a place ....

b) Mineral water without gas ....

c) It tells you how much you have to pay........................
(Note: all the words are in the text on this page.)

Read and notice

Read notices that you see in your workplace.

Read adverts in newspapers and look for the same words.

Look for websites advertising jobs or advertising hotels.

Think about the spelling

1 Find the words

Read the texts on the facing page and underline all the words with a double consonant at the end.

Find four words ending in 'ss'.

Find four words ending in 'll'.

Find one word ending in 'nn'.

Find one word ending in 'zz'.

Find one word ending in 'ff'.

2 Look and learn

a) Write these words in groups according to the consonants at the end (write the double consonants in a different colour from the rest of the word).

What are the consonants at the end?				
ss	ll	nn	zz	ff
address				

b) **Notice**: How many vowel letters come immediately before the double consonants? *one*

c) Look at the pictures and write the word under it. Then circle the double letters at the end.

bi(ll)					

grass   boss   kiss   bill   pull   chess

3 Listen and learn

Listen to some words with a double consonant at the end in Audio 7.1. Notice the vowel sound. Double consonants often come after short vowel sounds, but not always. Listen to the words 'glass' and 'staff'. They have a longer vowel sound on this audio. Listen to the word 'waitress'. It has a shorter vowel sound.   🎧 **7.1**

Be careful

Not all words have a double consonant; e.g. 'hotel', 'yes'.

Practise the spelling

1 Listen and write the missing word in each sentence. 🎧 **7.2**

  a) I go to an English ....two days a week.

  b) 'Do you .... Chinese noodles?' 'I'm sorry, we don't.'

  c) I .... my old home.

  d) I don't know where I can find the money to pay this ....

  e) 'Can I go home? I don't feel very ....'

  f) Don't push the door. ....it.

  g) It's difficult to work if your .... is unfriendly.

  h) The favourite game in my family is ....

2 Circle the last three letters in these words, then put the words in pairs with the last three letters the same.

class	kill	sell	full	grass	chess	cross
miss	kiss	bill	pull	address	boss	well

e.g.   class and grass

3 Rhymes

  a) Words rhyme when they have the same sound at the end of the word. Look at these words and try to find two or more words that rhyme with them.

grass	class, glass, pass
kill	
well	

  b) Look at this rhyme. It could be from a song:

  After the class
  We sat on the grass

  Can you make a rhyme with a different pair of words?

4 Listen again to Audio 7.1 and write the words you hear. 🎧 **7.1**

Write

1 Choose four or five words with a double consonant at the end, and write four or five sentences (one for each word).

2 Imagine you work in a restaurant. Write a notice for staff or for guests. If you can work on a computer, try to make it look professional.

Learn how to learn

Learn by hearing

Do you remember things well if you hear them?

You can try different ways to remember spellings.

- Say the word out loud and say the names of the letters.

  beautiful   b – e – a – u – t – i – f – u – l

- Say the word out loud and say the letters that are difficult to remember.

  beautiful   e – a – u

- Try saying this over and over again.

  beautiful   e – a – u, beautiful   e – a – u, beautiful, e – a – u

- Ask someone to test you. They say the word and you say the names of the letters in the word.

- You can remember a particularly difficult word or an important word if you sing it!
  Make a little tune and sing the word and the letters you use to spell it.

- Make rhymes with words that have the same sound and the same spelling pattern, e.g.

After the class
We sat on the grass

UNIT 8
Comparing people and places

Double consonants

 Please refer to track 25 on the audio CD for this unit.

Read two people's writing about their experience.

Comparing people

" I am one of three sisters, and we all look different. My older sister is very tall. I am a bit shorter than her and my younger sister is very short.

I think that my sisters are slim, but the younger one thinks she is too fat. She always says she is fatter than me, but I don't think she is. My older sister is certainly slimmer than me. She is the slimmest person in the family. "

Comparing places

" I was born in a small town in Central Africa, but now I live in England. The places are very different. My town in England is much bigger than my town in Africa, and there are more things to buy and things to do, but I am not sure that life here is better.

The weather is also different. Of course, Africa is hotter than England, but I like the English weather sometimes. It can be hot in July or August, but it is not usually too hot. Sometimes England can be very wet, for example in March or April, but in the rainy season in my country, it can be even wetter than in England. "

Think about the meaning

Answer the questions below.

a) Which sister is shorter, the older or the younger?

b) Which sister is slimmer, the older or the younger?

c) Which town is bigger, in Africa or in England?

d) Which place is hotter, Africa or England?

e) When is the African town wetter than the town in England?

Read and notice

Read about other countries in student magazines.

Choose a country that interests you and search on the Internet for information about it.

Think about the spelling

1 Find the words

a) Look at the text on the facing page and underline the comparative of these adjectives:
young, short, old, hot, slim, fat, wet, big.

e.g. younger hotter

b) What is the comparative of 'good'? Find it in the text.

2 Look and learn

a) Write the comparative forms here and draw a circle around the double letters:

young.........younger ....   hot ....hotter.........................
short...............................   slim..
old...............................   fat..
        wet ....
        big ....

Notice: How many vowel letters and how many consonant letters are at the end of the words
'hot', 'slim', 'fat', 'wet' and 'big'?

When do you double the consonant to make the comparative?

b) Now make the comparatives of these words.

Adjective	thin	cold	fit	fast
Comparative				

c) Look at the 'ing' form of two verbs 'run' and 'work'.

Run: I run every day
Running: I love running
Work: I work in an office
Working: I am not working today

Look at this list of verbs below. Look carefully at the number of vowel letters and the number of
consonant letters at the end, and write them in two columns, like the example.

run, swim, cut, work, send, jog, begin, meet, jump, sit, rain

+ 'ing'	double the last consonant + 'ing'
work – work**ing**	run – ru**nn**ing

3 Listen and learn

Listen to the words in Audio 8.1. Notice the <u>first</u> vowel sound in each word.
You will hear a short vowel sound every time.

 8.1

Be careful

Double consonants usually only happen after a short vowel sound.

Practise the spelling

1 Read these sentences below:

'I <u>run</u> in the park every day.' 'I like <u>running</u> in the park.'

> Write a second sentence, using the 'ing' form like the example, for each of these sentences:
>
> a) I sit in my garden every morning.
>
> b) I jog one mile every day.
>
> c) I swim three times a week.

2 Look at this example:

'A person who jogs' – 'a <u>jogger</u>'

Find the right words and add them to the crossword grid.

All of them have double letters.

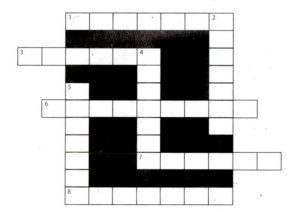

Across

1 A person who swims.
3 The person who comes first in a race.
6 People who start to learn something.
7 It comes after spring and before autumn.
8 Not so fat.

Down

2 People who rob (steal from other people).
4 People who run.
5 There are 26 in the alphabet.

3 Listen again to Audio 8.1 and write the words you hear.   **8.1**

Write

Write some sentences comparing people you know and places you know.

Remember to write capital letters for the names.

Learn how to learn

Learn by doing

Do you remember things well if you do something with your hands?

You can try different ways to remember spellings.

- Write the word again and again. Make sure you write it correctly.

  weather   weather   weather

- Write the word in the air with your hand.

- Take a piece of tracing paper (paper you can see through).
  Cover the word with the tracing paper and copy the word. The word needs to be quite big if you want to do this.

- When you write, always make sure you do 'joined up writing'. When you join up your letters, each letter runs into the next letter. In time, this can help you to remember spellings. If you have difficulty with joined up writing, it will help you to use a handwriting practice book.

- If you like, you can use your fingers to count out the number of letters in a word. This can help you with your spelling.

  w – e – a – t – h – e – r

- You can use plastic letters and move them around to make words.

- Write a word on card and cut it into separate letters, then move the letters around to make the word again.

- Use a computer. Type the word into a word-processing program. Use the spell-check to find out if it is correct.

UNIT 9
Money

Vowels: silent 'e' with 'a'

 Please refer to tracks 26–36 on the audio CD for this unit.

Read the notices below.

1 END OF SEASON SALE
    50% off many items
	2 Save up to £100 on a new computer. Hurry,
	    offer ends soon. Click **here** for details

3 Please take your cash	4 The Governor of the Bank of England said today that the interest rate will go up

5 Click **here** to see your current statement
    Click **here** to see your previous statement
	6 MAKE MONEY IN YOUR FREE TIME EARN
	    £££ WORKING FROM HOME

Think about the meaning

1 Which of the above notices could you find:

   a) on a shop window?

   b) on a cash machine?

   c) on the website for an online shop?

   d) on a leaflet given out in the street?

   e) in a newspaper?

   f) on an online banking site?

2 Match the word with the meaning.

Interest	Money in the hand (paper money or coins)
Statement	A time when shops sell things more cheaply
Sale	If you borrow money, you pay back more; for example, 2% or 5%
Cash	The bank tells you (on paper or on the Internet) how much money you have in your account

Read and notice

Read notices around you, on machines and on shop windows.

Look for websites for shops and banks.

Think about the spelling

In some words, the vowel sound is made with two vowel letters, but they are not together in the word. There is an 'e' at the end of the word, but you don't hear the 'e' when you say the word. This is sometimes called a 'silent e'.

1 Find the words

Underline these words in the notices on the facing page. They all have a 'silent e':
sale; save; rate; make; take; statement

2 Look and learn

a) Look at all these words with the same spelling pattern. Check that you understand the meaning.

> sale; save; rate; make; take
>
> name; cake; brave; female; same; place; race; late; plate, face

b) Group all the words so that the letter between 'a' and 'e' is the same.

When you write the words, write 'a' under 'a' and 'e' under 'e'.

This can help you remember the pattern.

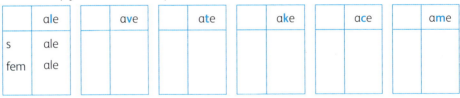

	ale		ave		ate		ake		ace		ame
s	ale										
fem	ale										

Try to remember these words in groups, with the same spelling pattern.

3 Listen and learn

a) Look at the words in **2** and listen at the same time to Audio 9.1.   🎧 **9.1**

b) Read and listen to these pairs of words   🎧 **9.2**

(1) mad – (2) made   (1) Sam – (2) same   (1) fat – (2) fate

Notice the difference the 'e' makes to the sound of the word.

c) Read and listen to these pairs of words below. Notice the 'k' and the 'c' and notice the consonant sound: 🎧 **9.3**

(1) take cake make

(2) place race face

Can you think of other words ending in 'ake' and 'ace'?

Be careful

One very common word has the same spelling pattern, but a different sound. This word is 'have'.

Listen to these words in Audio 9.4:

save, gave, wave, cave and have   🎧 **9.4**

Not all words with this sound have this spelling pattern, e.g. 'train'.

Practise the spelling

1 Listen to Audio 9.5 and fill the gaps in the sentences.   **9.5**

  a) We watched a bicycle ....

  b) Your baby has a lovely ....

  c) .... care.

  d) Don't .... a noise.

  e) Try not to .... the baby.

  f) He's looking for a .... to live.

2 Put these words in pairs with the last three letters the same; e.g. 'late' and 'gate'.

game	gate	place	name	make	cake	sale
face	page	save	age	late	pale	gave

3 Put a suitable word from the list above in each gap.

  a. My mother ....me some money for my birthday.

  b. He has a thin ....and long, black hair.

  c. I started school at the ....of six.

  d. Can you ....sandwiches for the children's lunch?

  e. Please open the book at ....23.

  f. I love chocolate ....

  g. I can't remember his ....

4 Make rhymes.

  Read this rhyme below and try to make your own from the pairs of words above.

They got there too late

So we closed the gate

5 Listen again to Audio 9.1 and write the words you hear.   **9.1**

Write

Choose four or five words with the 'a-e' spelling pattern, and write four or five sentences (one for each word).

Imagine you work in a shop.

Write a notice for customers, either for the shop window or for the website.

Learn how to learn

Letters and sounds

English does not have a simple way of relating letters to sounds. If your language is not English, you may need to practise hearing the difference between some sounds. This is because your own language does not have exactly the same sounds as English.

1 Consonants

Can you hear the difference between consonant sounds?

Read and listen to these pairs of words.   🎧 **9.6**

a) pin – bin

b) best – vest

c) fan – van

d) pan – fan

e) vest – west

f) nine – line

Listen to Audio 9.7.   🎧 **9.7**

You will hear only one word of each pair. Underline the word you hear.

2 Vowels

Can you hear the difference between short vowel sounds?

Read and listen to these pairs of words.   🎧 **9.8**

a) pan – pen

b) pen – pin

c) cat – cut

d) boss – bus

Listen to Audio 9.9.   🎧 **9.9**

You will hear only one word of each pair. Underline the word you hear.

3 Listen to these words. You will hear 19 different vowel sounds.   🎧 **9.10**

again	hand	road	car	right
see	bus	soon	rain	boy
big	hot	put	near	now
leg	law	girl	where	

Sometimes it is difficult to link spelling with pronunciation, because in different parts of the country, people have a different pronunciation. This is especially true with vowels. If you are interested in this idea, listen to these words again.   🎧 **9.11**

again	hand	road	car	right
see	bus	soon	rain	boy
big	hot	put	near	now
leg	law	girl	where	

The pronunciation you hear in Audio 9.10 is the standard pronunciation. Listen to Audio 9.11 to hear someone from Scotland saying the same words. What differences in vowel sounds do you hear?

Bank accounts

Vowels: silent 'e' with 'o'

 Please refer to tracks 37–40 on the audio CD for this unit.

Read the conversation below.

Anna:	"I phoned yesterday and spoke to somebody about my account. I want to close my old account and open a new high rate account. They said that's possible".
Bank employee:	"Yes, it is. What's your account number?"
Anna:	"50673421."
Bank employee:	"And your name?"
Anna:	"Jones. A Jones".
Bank employee:	"And a couple of security questions – what's your date of birth?"
Anna:	"29.6.75."
Bank employee:	"And your mother's maiden name?"
Anna:	"Morgan."
Bank employee:	"Fine. I'll close your old account, then if you fill in this form, you can open your new account and transfer the money."

Now read the form that Anna filled in below.

XYZ BANK – APPLICATION TO OPEN AN ACCOUNT	
Surname:	Jones
Other name:	Anna
Home address:	86 Hyde Park Lane
	Leeds
Postcode:	LS6 3DU
Phone:	0113 356 9826 (home)
	(work)
	(mobile)

Think about the meaning

1 What does she want to close?
2 What does she want to open?
3 What is her home phone number?
4 What is her postcode?
5 Does she have a mobile phone?

What is the past tense of these words?
phone; open; close; speak

Read and notice

Read leaflets and forms you find in banks.

Look on the website of a bank, download a form and read it.

Think about the spelling

1 Find the words

Find and highlight these words in the text on the facing page:

> phoned; spoke; close; open; home; code; phone; Jones

Look at the text again, find these words and highlight them in a different colour:

> rate; name; lane; date

The pattern is similar. The first group of words uses silent 'e' with 'o'.
The second group uses silent 'e' with 'a'.

2 Look and learn

a) Use a word-processing program to make this pattern: – o – e

Copy and paste until you have about ten copies.

Find words to fit the pattern and type in the missing letters, or print the pattern and write the letters in by hand.

b) Look at the text on the facing page again, and choose a few words you want to learn to spell. Or think of words you need to write when you fill in a form. Use 'look – cover – write – check' to help you learn them (see p. 17).

3 Listen and learn

a) Listen to the words in **1** above.   **10.1**

b) Listen to the pronunciation of these pairs of words.   **10.2**

> 1 hop – 2 hope   1 not – 2 note

Notice how the 'e' changes the pronunciation. The silent 'e' makes the 'o' have the same vowel sound as its own name.

c) Look at the spelling of these two words:

> post; old

The vowel sound is the same as 'phone', 'home', etc., but there is no 'e'. Why do you think there is no 'e'?

Be careful

A lot of common words have the same '– o – e' spelling pattern as the words in this unit, but a different pronunciation; e.g. one, come, love, some, lose. Listen to the pronunciation of these words in Audio 10.3.   **10.3**

Practise the spelling

1 Look at this list of words below.

rose	joke	hope	close	whole	smoke	home
phone	bone	rope	nose	hole	alone	

Look at the pictures and choose one word from the list for each picture.

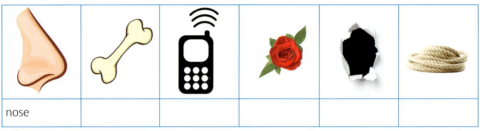

nose					

2 Look at the list of words in **1** again. Put one word in each of the gaps. You may have to add 's' to make a word plural.

a) I arrived .... very late last night.

b) My friend lives .... in a small flat.

c) I lost some money because there is a .... in my pocket.

d) My uncle is very funny. He tells lots of ....

e) He had an accident and broke a .... in his foot.

f) .... are my favourite flowers.

3 Two of the words in the list in **1** above have exactly the same pronunciation.

Which ones are they?

Listen to Audio 10.4 and write one of these two words in each sentence.   **10.4**

a) There was a .... in the road and I fell over.

b) My .... family came to visit.

c) My father lived his .... life in the same house.

d) I lost my wallet because there was a .... in my pocket.

4 Use a grammar book to find the past tense of the verbs in these sentences, then change the sentences to the past.

a) They <u>speak</u> Spanish   *They spoke Spanish*

b) We <u>break</u> the record

c) They <u>steal</u> things from their workplace

d) I <u>wake</u> up early

e) I <u>ride</u> my bike to work

5 Listen again to Audio 10.1 and write the words you hear.   **10.1**

Write

Choose four or five words with the '– o – e' pattern and write a sentence for each word.

Find forms from banks and other official places and fill them in.

Learn how to learn

Which words to learn?

When you start to work on spelling, you cannot learn too many words at one time. Choose which ones to learn first.

Some words are very common and it is a good idea to learn to spell them, because you need to write them a lot. For example, 'always', 'because', 'again'. Other words are not so common; for example, 'originally'.

Some words are important for you personally. For example, the word 'receptionist' is not very common, but if you are a receptionist, then it is an important word for you. You need to write it when you fill in a form.

1 Read this piece of student writing. The student made 20 spelling mistakes and the teacher corrected them. (All the words in blue are correct now, but they were the student's mistakes.) Choose eight words only for the student to learn first. Which are the most useful words for the student to learn? Which ones are common words that come again and again? Which are important personal words for the student?

My name is Ala and I come from Poland. Now I live with my husband and children in a flat near the centre of Liverpool. When we first came to England, my husband worked as a builder, but I didn't have a job. However, my English is better now and I have a job as a cashier in a supermarket. I enjoy the job and am pleased that I can earn some money.

I have one English friend. Her name is Jane and she lives near me. Jane comes originally from Durham. She came here to study in university and she didn't go back. She is a librarian and works in the public library. I sometimes meet her when she finishes work and we go for a coffee together.

One day soon Jane and I are planning to go on a trip to the Lake District. It's a part of Britain I would really like to see.

2 a) Think of words that are important for you personally.

b) Think of words you need to write when you fill in a form.

c) Think of words that are useful for your job.

d) Think of words that help you to write about your interests.

Find the correct spelling of some of these words, and write them down.

Look at your own writing and ask someone to underline spelling mistakes. Choose five or six words to work on. Choose words because they are common words, or because they are important for you personally.

3 Use 'look, cover, write, check' (see page 17) to learn the words you decided to learn.

Restaurants

Vowels: silent 'e' with 'i'

 Please refer to tracks 41–46 on the audio CD for this unit.

Read this newspaper advertisement for a restaurant.

Porter's Restaurant

Try our new lunchtime menu

2 courses for only £8.95

Chicken supreme

Chicken in a delicious white wine sauce,
with fine green beans and baby new potatoes

Vegetable curry

A vegetable curry with coconut (choose hot,
medium or mild), with mango chutney,
lime pickle and rice

Spicy Chinese beef

Beef cooked with tomatoes and spices, with
stir-fry vegetables and noodles or rice

Cheese, onion and tomato pie

A vegetarian dish made with fresh vegetables,
served with a side salad

❖❖❖❖

Exotic fruit salad

Fruit salad with mango and pineapple

Apple pie

A delicious apple pie, with cream or ice cream

Think about the meaning

1 Raj is a vegetarian. What can he eat?

Sonia doesn't like spicy food. What can she eat?

2 What would you like to eat in this restaurant?

I would like ....

I wouldn't like...

Say why you would like or wouldn't like certain things.

Read and notice

Read things in newspapers and magazines about food or restaurants.

Read recipes.

Find restaurant menus or recipes on the Internet.

Think about the spelling

1 Find the words

Find the words below in the menu on the facing page. Highlight them.

time; white; wine; fine; spices; rice; lime; side; pineapple; ice; pie

In what way is the word 'pie' different from the others?

2 Look and learn

Take two different coloured pens and copy the words above, with the vowels in one colour and the consonants in another, e.g.:

t i m e   w h i t e

Notice the pattern of the vowels.

3 Listen and learn

a) Listen to this list of words with the '– i – e' pattern in Audio 11.1.   **11.1**

b) Listen to the pairs of words below. **11.2**

1 win – 2 wine   1 Tim – 2 time   1 bit – 2 bite

Notice how the 'e' changes the pronunciation. The silent 'e' makes the 'i' have the same vowel sound as it has in its own name.

c) Notice different vowel sounds. **11.3**

Read these pairs of words.

1 race – 2 rice   1 lake – 2 like   1 male – 2 mile

One word has the '– a – e' sound, and one word has the '– i – e' sound.

Read the sentences and listen at the same time.

Notice the vowel sounds in the 'a-e' words and the '– i – e' words.

a) We went to watch a cycle <u>race</u>.

b) A lot of <u>rice</u> grows in China.

c) There is a very big <u>lake</u> in Africa, called Lake Victoria.

d) I <u>like</u> Indian food.

e) I have a new cat. It's a <u>male</u>.

f) I walk a <u>mile</u> to work every day.

4 Listen to the single words in Audio 11.4 and say which sentence they come from (a, b, c, d, e or f).   **11.4**

5 Look at the words below. They are in the advertisement on page 42.

try; fry; mild

They have the same vowel sound as the '– i – e' words, but different spelling patterns. Listen to these other words with the same patterns:

a) try; fry; cry; fly; dry   b) mild; wild; kind; find   **11.5**

Be careful

Some very common words have the same spelling pattern, but a different pronunciation, e.g. 'give' and 'live'.

Practise the spelling

1 Listen to Audio 11.6 and fill the gaps in the following text   🎧 **11.6**

In Europe, many people drink .... with a meal. They usually drink red .... with red meat, such as beef, and .... with .... meat, such as chicken, or with fish. With vegetarian food, they .... drink red, ... as they ....

In Australia, people .... to drink beer, ... cold, and in Japan there is a local .... made from.............. .

Of course, many people never drink alcohol. If you travel in Asia, you can find very .... fruit cocktails, made from mango, ... oranges or .... Or why not try .... tea or coffee, when the weather is hot. It's delicious.

2 Find a word that fits the pattern 'i-e', with the following meanings:

a) It belongs to me ....*mine.*.........

b) A woman I am married to ....

c) A clock tells it to you ....

d) Everything is OK ....

e) You open this when you want to use your computer ....

f) More than one mouse ....

g) This is just over two kilometres ....

h) A small green fruit, like a lemon ....

i) The opposite of black ....

3 Listen again to Audio 11.1 and write the words you hear.   🎧 **11.1**

Write

Write about the food and drink that you like.

Learn how to learn

Split words into parts

1 If you want to remember how to spell a long word, you can break it up into syllables.

A syllable is a part of a word with its own vowel sound.

For example:
- Name   has one syllable
- Address   has two syllables
- Telephone   has three syllables

Say the words aloud and hear the different syllables. Count the syllables on your fingers.

If you want to learn to spell a long word, it can help if you break it up.

Sometimes, the long word has other real words inside.

yesterday

yes   ter   day

If you can spell the short words **yes** and **day**, it can help you with the long word.

Other words do not have real words inside them, but you can still break them into syllables, e.g.

September

Sometimes, you can choose where to split a word. For example, you can split the word 'September' like this:

Sep   tem   ber   because it is in three equal parts.

Or you can split it like this:

Sept   ember   because that helps you remember that the ending is
                                       like the ending in 'November' and 'December' (and
                                       'remember').

2 Read these words below and decide where to split them to learn the spellings below:

tomorrow	sometimes	expensive	computer	together	coconut
restaurant	Saturday	different	example	vegetarian	tomato

Choose four or five of these words and learn how to spell them.

UNIT 12
Driving lessons

Dropping silent 'e'

 Please refer to tracks 47–48 on the audio CD for this unit.

Read the online advert for a driving school below, then read the form that Sabir Khan filled in below that.

Are you learning to drive?
Or are you thinking about it?

- The Harbour Driving School
- Very high success rate
- Intensive Driving Courses
- Reasonable prices

Our intensive driving courses are each for one week, Monday to Friday.

Courses start every 2 weeks.

Book now!

Name:	Sabir Khan

Address:	35 Anderson Street, Portsmouth
Postcode:	PO6 5JQ

When would you like to start your course?

2nd July   (16th July)   30th July   13th August   27th August

Tell us something about your driving experience?

I had my first driving lesson three weeks ago. I had three lessons in June, and am going to have two more before your course begins. I am taking my theory test on the 12th of July, and I am hoping to take my practical test in August.

Think about the meaning

Answer the questions below.

1 What is the name of the driving school?
2 How long do the driving courses last?
3 When did Sabir Khan start driving lessons?
4 When is he taking his theory test?
5 When does he want to take his practical test?

Read and notice

Read online adverts.

Think about the spelling

1 Find the words

Read the advert and the form on the facing page and underline all the 'ing' forms.

Look at the base form of these verbs.

What is the 'ing' form?

Base form	'ing' form
learn	learning
drive	
go	
hope	
take	
think	

Notice: What happens to the words that end in 'e'?

2 Look and learn

Here is how to remember to leave off the 'e':

a) Write the base word very big, then take a pen and draw a big cross through the 'e' before you write the 'ing', like this:

drив̸ + ing

b) Take some small pieces of paper and a pair of scissors. Write the base word on one piece of paper, write 'ing' on the other, then physically cut off the 'e' from the base word before you join it to the 'ing'.

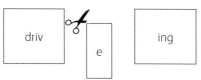

Write the 'ing' form of some of the words above, then draw a circle around the last four letters, to help you think of them as a group, like this:

driving

3 Listen and learn

Listen to the 'ing' forms of some of these verbs. **12.1**

Be careful

Notice the difference in pronunciation between a word where the silent 'e' was lost and another word which had no silent 'e':

1 hopping – 2 hoping

Listen to the pronunciation of this pair of words in Audio 12.2. **12.2**

Practise the spelling

1 Read the first sentence and complete the others below.

   a) A person who drives is a driver

   b) A person who writes is a ....

   c) A person who bakes is a ....

   d) A person who smokes is a ....

   e) A person who dances is a ....

2 Look at the words below and write the 'ing' form.

drive	write	hope	make	take
have	phone	come	close	give
shine	smile	dance	joke	shave

3 Write a sentence to describe what is happening in each picture. Use some of the words in the box above.

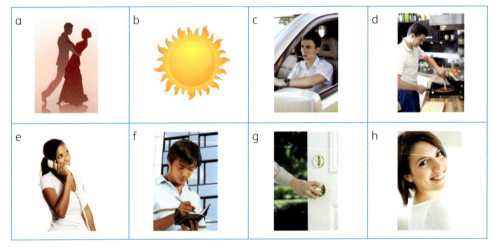

   a) They ....

   b) The sun ....

   c) He ....

   d) He ....the dinner....

   e) She ....her friend

   f) He ....

   g) She ....the door

   h) She ....

4 Listen again to Audio 12.1 and write the words you hear.   **12.1**

Write

Fill in a form online to book a place or to order something (make sure you stop before they take your money!).

Learn how to learn

Count the letters

Before you learn to spell a long word, count the letters.

How many letters are there in:

DRIVING

SCHOOL

INFORMATION

Make a note of the number of letters and try to write the word. Count the letters in your word.

Make a test for yourself.

Copy the word you want to learn, but first leave out the consonants.

information

i - - o - - a - i o -

Cover the correct spelling and try to fill the gaps.

Check your spelling against the correct spelling.

Then copy the same word, but leave out the vowels.

- n f - r m - t - - n

Cover the correct spelling and try to fill the gaps.

Check your spelling against the correct spelling.

Finally, count the number of letters and draw a gap for each letter

- - - - - - - - - - -

Cover the correct spelling and try to fill the gaps.

Check your spelling against the correct spelling.

In the town

Vowel sound 'ar'

 Please refer to track 49 on the audio CD for this unit.

Look at the map below.

Think about the meaning

Write about all the places you can see on the map.

The ....is next to the ....

The ....is opposite the ....

The ....is near the ....

Read and notice

As you walk around the area where you live, look at the signs on the buildings and notice the spelling.

Choose any town in an English speaking country and download a local area map. Look for some of these places on it.

Think about the spelling

1 Find the words

Look at the map again on the facing page.

How many of the words on the map have 'ar' in them?

Underline all the words with 'ar'.

2 Look and learn

a) Write all these 'ar' words with the 'ar' in a different colour from the other letters, e.g.

c**ar** p**ar**k

b) Write the words under the pictures. When you have finished, draw a circle around the letters 'ar'.

c) Draw your own map, but draw in only places with 'ar' in their name. When you finish the map, draw a circle round the letters 'ar' in each word.

d) Look at some of the longer words on the map on the facing page.

Split them into syllables, e.g.

su / per / mark / et   or   de / part / ment

Now look for words inside words, e.g.

s u p e r m a r k e t

mark is a real word

Can you find real words inside these words?

pharmacy   department

Split the words into syllables and use 'look – cover – write – check' (see page 17) to help you to learn the words.

3 Listen and learn

Listen to some words with 'ar' and read them on the map.   **13.1**

Be careful

There are many words with similar pronunciation which are not spelt with 'ar'; e.g., 'bath', 'father', 'pass', 'past'.

Sometimes the letters 'ar' together are part of a different spelling pattern, with a different pronunciation; e.g. 'care', 'parents'.

Practise the spelling

1

SUPERMARKET 100 METRES	CAR PARK 500 metres
GARDEN CENTRE 2 KM	SNACK BAR round the corner
CHILDREN'S PLAY PARK 100 metres	FARMERS' MARKET for fresh fruit and vegetables 100 metres

Make questions with 'how far...?'

Write the questions and the answers, e.g.

'How far is the supermarket?' '100 metres'

2 A puzzle

Find the word that fits the meaning. All the words have 'ar' in them.

When you have finished, an extra word appears down the middle.

1) February, ..., April.
2) Part of the body, between the shoulder and hand.
3) You can send it to people on their birthdays.
4) If you invite a lot of people, you can have a good ....
5) Small, medium, ...
6) The opposite of 'finish'.

3 Listen again to Audio 13.1 and write the words you hear.   **13.1**

Write

Choose some words from the unit, and write one sentence for each word.

Make a map of your own area.

Write about your area, describe places and write about where they are.

Write about what you like and don't like about the area.

Learn how to learn

How important is correct spelling?

Is it always important to spell correctly?

Think of the situations below and decide how important it is to be correct.

- Sending an email to a friend.
- Writing a formal letter.
- Writing a telephone message at work.
- Writing a note for your brother.
- Writing an exam.

Some mistakes in spelling are serious, some are not so serious.

Look at how different students spell the word 'CHICKEN' below:
None of the students spells the word correctly.

The correct spelling is 'chicken'.

Student A writes 'chikin'.

Student B writes 'ciken'.

Student C writes 'kichen'.

Student D writes 'chickin'.

Student E writes 'cecn'.

Can you read and understand what the students want to write? If you cannot understand, the mistake is serious. If the spelling is not perfect, but you know which word the student wants to write, it is not so serious. Tick the box with your opinion.

	The mistake is serious. I cannot understand the word	The mistake is not so serious. I can understand the word
Student A		
Student B		
Student C		
Student D		
Student E		

Take a piece of your own writing. Underline the words you spelled wrong. Ask another person to tell you if they can understand which word you wanted to write. Decide how serious your mistakes are.

In which situations will you try to make sure your spelling is absolutely correct?

'all'

 Please refer to tracks 50–53 on the audio CD for this unit.

Read this advert in a newspaper for a holiday park.

Come and stay at Riverside Holiday Park

The park is set in beautiful countryside. Take a walk through the woods or along the river bank to the waterfall. Or relax in our lovely flower gardens.

We have a large sports hall for badminton, table tennis and basketball. We also have a well-equipped gym, tennis courts and a football pitch.

For younger children, there is always lots to do. We have toys, play parks, with bouncy castle and ball pit, and lots of fun activities.

We even have a small animal zoo.

With comfortable rooms, good restaurants, cafes and bars, Riverside Holiday Park is perfect for all the family.

For more information call **0800** ‑‑‑‑‑‑‑‑‑ Or visit **www.Riverhols.com**

Think about the meaning

Carmen and Luis want to go on holiday with their two children and Carmen's mother.

Carmen and Luis like walking in the countryside.

Their son Jose is 12 years old, and likes sport.

Their daughter Ana is five years old.

Carmen's mother is not very strong.

1 What do you think each person will like best in Riverside Holiday Park?

What will Carmen and Luis want to do?

What will Jose want to do?

What will Ana want to do?

What will Carmen's mother want to do?

2 Would you like to go to a holiday park like this one?

If so, what would you like to do there?

Read and notice

Read leaflets and adverts for places to visit.

Look on the Internet for details in English of holiday places, in the country where you are or in another country.

Think about the spelling

1 Find the words

Find and underline these words in the text on the facing page:

call; small; waterfall; football; basketball; hall; all; ball; also; always

2 Look and learn

a) Use a word-processing program to make this pattern: ....all

Copy and paste until you have about ten copies.

Find words to fit the pattern and type in the missing letters, or print the pattern and write the letters in by hand.

b) Circle the first two letters of the three words below:

also   always   already

3 Listen and learn

i) Read the words below and listen at the same time.   **14.1**

all   ball   call   fall   hall   small   tall   wall   also
always   already

ii) Listen to the words 'walk' and 'talk'. The vowel sound is the same as the vowel sound in
'wall' and 'tall'.   **14.2**

iii) Hear the difference between two sounds.

Read and listen to these words and sentences:

1 hall   2 hole   **14.3**
1 walk   2 woke

a) The college has a new sports <u>hall</u>.

b) There's a <u>hole</u> in my pocket.

c) I usually <u>walk</u> to college.

d) I <u>woke</u> up early this morning.

3 Listen to the single words and say which sentence they come from (a, b, c or d)   **14.4**

Be careful!

There are many other ways to write the same vowel sound.

Practise the spelling

1 Write a word that fits the meaning. All of them end in 'all'.

A round object – there are many games you can play with it	
The opposite of 'big'	
Every building needs four or more of these	
Speak to someone on the phone	

2 Read these words, then put the right word in each gap.

wall, fall, hall, call, stall, tall, ball, small, football

a) Basketball players are usually very ....

b) .... me if you have any problems.

c) There are three new courts in the badminton ....

d) In a game of squash, you hit the ....against a ....

e) Look after .... children in the play park. Make sure they don't ....

f) When you finish playing ...., you can buy food and drink at the refreshment
....

3 Write one of these words below in each gap.

also   always   already

a) He loves football, but he .... plays cricket and tennis.

b) We expected him to arrive at 3 o'clock, but it's only 2 o'clock, and he's here ....

c) She .... arrives early or on time, never late.

4 Listen again to Audio 14.1 and write the words you hear.   **14.1**

Write

Write an advert to encourage people to visit a place you know and like.

Read and notice

What do you read as you go about your daily life?

There is a lot to read everywhere we go.

Sometimes you can expect the spelling to be correct, but in some situations it is not always correct.

Think about the following things you can read.

	I expect the spelling to be correct	The spelling may not always be correct
A newspaper		
Printed posters outside supermarkets		
Handwritten posters outside shops		
Company websites		
A novel		
An email to a friend		
Signs on a railway station platform		
Adverts in a magazine		
Adverts in a newsagent's window		
Postings on social networking sites		

You can read and notice spellings, but you need to know that not everything you read has correct spelling.

If you read a lot, it can help your spelling. You don't need to stop and think about it. Enjoy reading, and you can sometimes find your spelling is getting better.

What do you enjoy reading in English?

Supermarket shopping

Vowel sounds with 'ee' and 'ea'

 Please refer to tracks 54–56 on the audio CD for this unit.

Read this list of special offers in a supermarket.

THIS WEEKS SPECIAL OFFERS

Fresh green beans **2** *packets for the price of* **1**	**Baked beans (125 gram tin)** **Only 15p**
20% off **all French cheeses**	**3 for 2** **Tea bags**
Buy 2 tubs of chocolate ice cream and get a chocolate bar **FREE**	**LEAN MINCED BEEF** **350 grams for the price of 250**
Buy one, get one free **Mixed leaf salad**	**FREE** *frozen mixed vegetables* *when you buy a 1 kg packet of* *frozen garden peas*

IT'S CHEAPER TO SHOP HERE

Think about the meaning

What are the special offers on

- Meat? ....
- Fresh vegetables? ....
- Frozen foods? ....
- Other items? ....

Read and notice

Read notices outside supermarkets and read the labels on the food you buy.

Look on the Internet for supermarket websites.

Think about the spelling

1 Find the words

Make two lists of words from the notice on the facing page.

List all the words with 'ee' together and all the words with 'ea' together.

Words with 'ee'	Words with 'ea'
green	beans

2 Look and learn

a) Look at the word 'green'. It has the double 'e' spelling pattern. Take a green highlighter pen and highlight 'ee' in the words in your 'ee' list. Take an orange highlighter pen and highlight 'ea' in the words in your 'ea' list.

Now highlight 'ee' and 'ea' in these words below and add them to your lists (if they are not already there).

sleep	green	clean	see	eat	street
cheap	meal	tea	feel	please	cheese

b) Choose some words from the text on the facing page that you want to learn to spell. If they are long words, split them into syllables and look for other words inside them, e.g. 'vegetable' has the word 'table' inside. You can make a sentence: 'There are some vegetables on the table'.

Use 'look, cover, write, check' to learn to spell these words (see page 17).

3 Listen and learn

a) Listen to some of the words with the 'ee' and the 'ea' spelling. All the words have the same vowel sound.　 **15.1**

b) Hear the difference between this sound and another sound.　 **15.2**

Look at the pictures below, read the words and listen to Audio 15.2.

1 bin	2 bean	1 ship	2 sheep

c) Listen to the same words in a different order.　 **15.3**

When you hear a word, put your finger on the right picture.

Listen again, and write the words in the order you hear them.

Be careful

Some words have the same spelling, but different pronunciation, e.g. 'bread' rhymes with 'red'.

Some words have the same pronunciation exactly, but different spellings and different meanings, e.g.:

meet – I'm pleased to meet you   meat – I don't eat meat

see – I'll see you later   sea – I like swimming in the sea

Practise the spelling

1 Look at these words again.

sleep	green	clean	see	eat	street	cheap
	meal	tea	feel	please	cheese	

Choose words from the list to complete this dialogue.

"There's a new café in the main .... It's very good"

"Is it expensive?"

"No, it's very ...."

"What can you get there?"

"A cup of ....or coffee, cola, lemonade. You can get a full cooked .... or you can have sandwiches.
They have chicken sandwiches, but if you don't .... meat, there are ....or egg sandwiches."

2 Words rhyme when the <u>end</u> of the word sounds the same.

e.g. green – clean

'Green' rhymes with 'clean'. 'Meal' does not rhyme with 'meat'.

You often find rhymes in songs, e.g.

The grass was green
And the river was clean

You can see that the rhyming pairs can have a different spelling pattern. It is the sound that makes the rhyme, not the spelling.

Look at the list above again and find the word which rhymes with each of the words in the box.

green	clean
	eat
sleep	
see	
	meal
	please

Can you make rhymes from some of these words?

3 Listen again to Audio 15.1 and write the words you hear.   **15.1**

Write

Imagine you have a job in a small shop. The manager wants you to write a notice, showing the special offers. Write a notice to put in the shop window or to add to the shop's web page.

Learn how to learn

Use a dictionary

There are different kinds of dictionary, e.g.

- Complete English–English dictionary
- Learner's English–English dictionary
- Spelling dictionary
- Bilingual dictionary
- Electronic dictionary

Write the type of dictionary under the description.

1   This dictionary has the words, but not the meaning.

....

2   This dictionary is good for anyone who speaks English.

....

3   This dictionary has words in two languages.

....

4   This dictionary is a kind of hand-held computer.

....

5   This dictionary does not have very difficult words.

....

Which of these dictionaries do you have?

Which of them are in your library?

The library

Vowel sounds with 'oo'

 Please refer to tracks 57–59 on the audio CD for this unit.

Read these notices in a library.

AUDIO-VISUAL ROOM

Please book a time if you want to use a computer or watch a DVD

Are you looking for a good book to read?

Come and look in the school library

Choose any book you like

We have books on all subjects from computer science to cookery and are open from 9am to 5pm every day

---

Do not bring food and drink into the library

Switch **OFF** mobile phones

If the book you want is not in the library, you can order it.

Tell us and we will contact you as soon as it comes in.

Think about the meaning

Answer the questions below.

a) What are the opening times of the library?

b) What do you do if you want to watch a DVD?

c) If the book you want is not in the library, what can you do?

d) What is the rule about food and drink?

e) What is the rule about mobile phones?

Read and notice

Go to your library and read notices.

Then look for something which interests you to read – a book or magazine.

Find something to read in English in your local library.

Think about the spelling

1 Find the words

Read the notices on the facing page and underline all the words with 'oo'.

2 Look and learn

a) Write 'look' and draw two eyes inside the 'o's.

look

book

cook

Write 'book' and 'cook' under 'look'.

Remember the words as a group.

b) Look at these words below. Can you make pictures with the 'oo'? Here are some ideas:

school   sch◡◡l

food   f ● ● d

Can you do the same with these words?

zoo   foot   cook   moon

3 Listen and learn

Listen to two groups of words in Audio 16.1. Group (a) has a different vowel
sound to group (b) but the spelling is the same

good; book; look; cook; looking; cookery; foot

school; room; food; soon; zoo; choose

Can you hear the different vowel sounds?

🎧 **16.1**

Be careful

Lots of words with the same vowel sound as 'food' have a different spelling.

Listen to these sentences in Audio 16.2.

🎧 **16.2**

a) I like <u>fruit juice</u>. Do you like it?

b) He was very <u>rude</u> to me.

c) I have <u>two</u> sisters.

d) I want some <u>blue shoes.</u>

e) English does not have many clear spelling <u>rules.</u>

'fruit', 'juice', 'you', 'rude', 'two', 'blue', 'shoes' and 'rules' have the same vowel sound as 'food'
and 'school', but very different spelling.

'oo' is a fairly common spelling pattern for this sound, but there are many others.

Practise the spelling

1 Listen to Audio 16.3 and write the missing words. All of them have the
'oo' spelling   🎧 **16.3**

   a) Has anyone got any ……………………………? I'm really hungry.

   b) Let's go to the …………………..to see the animals.

   c) He hurt his …………………..in a running accident.

   d) That's a really …………………….idea.

   e) I like both of them. It's difficult to …………………….one.

   f) I left ……………….when I was 14.

   g) My sister works in a canteen. She's a …………………

2 Words rhyme when the <u>sound</u> at the end of the words is the same.

   Sometimes the spelling is very different, e.g., 'food' rhymes with 'rude'.

   Say these words aloud and put them into rhyming pairs:

   rude;   boot;   blue;   zoo;   school;   shoes;   food;
   choose;   fruit;   rule

rude	food

3 Sometimes, you can make funny or silly rhymes.

   Read this rhyme

   He was very rude
   He ate all the food

   Can you finish this rhyme:

   The sky is blue
   Let's go to the…………………………..

   Make other rhymes if you can.

4 Listen again to 16.1 and write the words you hear.   🎧 **16.1**

Write

Go to your library and get some information about it.

Then draw up a poster to encourage people to use it.

Learn how to learn

Find spellings in a dictionary

To find words in a dictionary, you need to be able to use alphabetical ordering quickly.

1 Put the words below in alphabetical order, as quickly as you can.

actor	van	town	daughter	eggs
glass	newspaper	cinema	hotel	jeans
fish	shop	quiz	yesterday	kitchen

2 Now put these words below in alphabetical order, as quickly as you can.

sell	street	station	September
sometimes	solicitor	Sunday	stop
spelling	son		

3 Find the spelling, if you know how the word begins.

Read these word beginnings, then look up the words in a dictionary. If you find more than one, choose one and write it down.

daug………   edu………………   tomo…………   indep……..

If you don't know how the word begins, you can guess. If the start of a word sounds like 's', try the letter 's'. If you can't find it, try the letter 'c'.

If you know the word in another language, you can use a bilingual dictionary. Find the word in the other language, then look for the English word you want.

The local council

vowel sounds with 'ou' and 'ow'

 Please refer to tracks 60–62 on the audio CD for this unit.

Read this leaflet about local councillors.

Your local councillors are:

Janet Greenwood, Mohammed Akram and James Moon

We are available to talk to you about the things that concern you, such as:

- Education
- Housing
- Safety in the community

Come along to
the South Building of the Council Offices
any
Tuesday or Friday, 6–8 pm

How to find us

Find the old Town Hall in the High Street. Go down the steps to the right of the Clock Tower on the outside of the building. Turn left and go round the corner of the Town Hall building. You will see the South Building in front of you.

Think about the meaning

Look at this diagram of the old Town Hall and the Council Offices.

Mark the South Building and how to get to it.

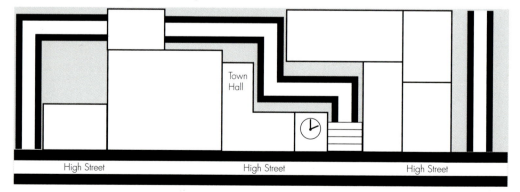

Read and notice

Read posters and leaflets from the local council.

Choose a town (maybe the town where you live or another one) and find information about the local council.

Think about the spelling

1 Find the words

Find and underline these words in the text on the facing page.

councillors   how   south   down   round   outside
council   about   town   housing   tower

2 Look and learn

a) List all the words with 'ow' together and all the words with 'ou' together.

Write 'ow' words in one colour, and 'ou' words in another colour.

Words with 'ow'	Words with 'ou'
how	councillors

b) Read these words below and add them to the table.

brown   mouse   town   found   pound   towel
loud   house   now   sound   flower

3 a) Split words to help remember them.

Look at these words below and decide how to split them into syllables.

outside   councillor   education   housing   available
building   community

e.g.   outside – out / side

councillor – coun / cil / lor

Notice: Look at the words 'house' and 'housing'.

What happens to the 'e'?

b) Choose three or four words from the facing page that you want to learn, and use 'look, cover, write, check' (page 17).

4 Listen and learn

a) Listen to these words with 'ow' and 'ou' in Audio 17.1. They all have the same vowel sound

 17.1

b) Listen to these two words: **17.2**

(1) flour   (2) flower

They sound exactly the same.

Use a dictionary to find out which one means:

i)   something you use for cooking

ii) something you see in the park or in a garden

Be careful

Many words with the 'ou' or 'ow' spelling have a different pronunciation from the ones here; e.g.

you   How are <u>you</u>?
young   She has a <u>young</u> son
slow   The bus is very <u>slow</u> today

Listen to Audio 17.3 to check the pronunciation   **17.3**

Practise the spelling

1 Read the words below and write one word in each gap.

mouse; found; pound; loud; house; sound; flower; town; now; towel

a) I ....a ....coin in the street.

b) There's a nice ....shop in the centre of ....

c) They are living in their new ....

d) I can't use the computer. I need to buy a new ....

e) Can you turn the radio down? It's too .... for me.

f) I'm going swimming. Where can I find a clean ....?

g) All the words in the gaps have the same vowel ....

2 A crossword puzzle

All the words <u>across</u> have 'ou' or 'ow' in them. The words <u>down</u> do not.

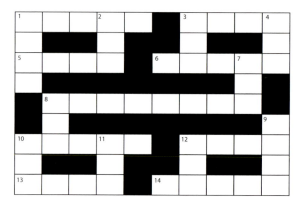

Across

1   British money

3   Animals that give us milk

5   Opposite of 'quiet'

6   A colour – some people have eyes this colour

8   Bigger than a hill

10 A part of the face, under the nose

12 Bigger than a village, smaller than a city

13 Opposite of 'up'

14 What you do when you say 1, 2, 3, 4 .....

Down

1   Don't push, ...

2   Move your head up and down

3   You can drive it

4   Not a daughter, a ....

7   What do you if you finish first in a race

8   The animals in 3 across say this

9   One part of the whole

10 Crazy, or very angry

11 Another word for a can, e.g. 'a can of tomatoes'

12 The number between one and three

3 Listen again to Audio 17.1 and write the words you hear.   **17.1**

Write

Write directions to tell someone how to find the place where you study or where you work.

Take care with the spelling of these words: about, how, down, round, outside

Learn how to learn

Work with a friend

If you write together with a friend, you can share the work of checking spelling.

- Discuss together what you want to write. Talk about any difficult words. Take it in turns to check the spelling.

- Work together on a computer. Discuss what you want to write. Decide together on the spelling of difficult words. Use the spell-check to know if you are right or not.

- Send emails to your friend. See if you can understand each other's meaning.

- Work with a friend to test each other.

  Take a list of words your friend is working on, and test him or her. Your friend can either write the words or say the spelling aloud.

- Make games and puzzles for each other.

  For example, take a few words and mix up the letters. Give this to your friend to sort out.

  Tell your friend the topic is 'buildings', then give him or her jumbled words like this:

  h s a t p o i l

  p r r s k e m u a t e

  o c o l h s

  Your friend can do the same for you with a different topic.

UNIT 18
Train travel

vowel sounds with 'ai' and 'ay'

 Please refer to tracks 63–68 on the audio CD for this unit.

Read these extracts from a website giving information about train travel.

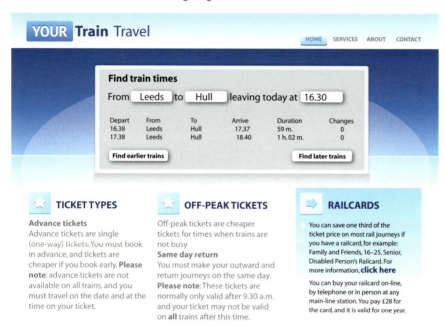

a) What time does the 16.38 train from Leeds arrive in Hull?

b) If you want to go somewhere for one day, what type of ticket can you buy?

c) If you buy an 'advance' ticket, can you travel on any train you like?

d) Where can you buy a railcard?

e) Is a railcard free?

Read and notice

Go online and find information about railcards.

Find out the following:

- How much do you pay for a railcard?
- How old is a person who can have a Senior Railcard?
- How many people can travel on a Family and Friends Railcard?
- What other types of railcard are there?
- How much money do you save if you have a railcard?

Think about the spelling

1 **Find the words**

   a) Find these words below in the text on the facing page and underline them.

      train   today   later   day   may   same   way   railcard

      main   pay   rail   save   make   available   date

   b) Then choose a colour and highlight these words:

      ==train, railcard, rail, available, main==

   c) Choose a second colour and highlight these words:

      ==today, day, may, way, pay==

2 **Look and learn**

Look at the words you highlighted, and write the words with 'ai' under the 'ai' column in a table as shown below. Write the words with 'ay' under the 'ay' column in a similar table. This can help you remember the pattern. Draw a circle around 'ai' and 'ay'.

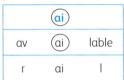

ai				ay	
av	(ai)	lable		tod	ay
r	ai	l			

Notice: When do you write 'ai' and when do you write 'ay'?

3 **Listen and learn**

   a) Read the words in the columns, then listen to Audio 18.1. There are two different spelling patterns, but the same vowel sound every time.

🎧 **18.1**

ay	ai
today	train
day	rail
may	railcard
way	available
pay	main

   b) Notice the difference between this vowel sound and another one.

🎧 **18.2**

     i)   pen: he had a pen in his hand (to write with).

     ii) pain: he had a pain in his hand (because he hurt his hand).

   c) Listen to the sentences again in a mixed up order in Audio 18.3. Write (i) or (ii) for each sentence you hear.

🎧 **18.3**

     (1) ......   (2) ......   (3)........   (4) ......   (5) ......   (6) ......

   d) Read and listen to these words from the text on the facing page. They have the 'a' + silent 'e' spelling (see Unit 9) but they have exactly the same vowel <u>sound</u> as the 'ai' and 'ay' words.

🎧 **18.4**

     later   save   same   make   date   take

Be careful

'Said' has 'ai' in the middle, but the pronunciation is different.

'He saw her in the street and said hello'.

🎧 **18.5**

Practise the spelling

1 What are these words? They all have 'ai' in them, but they are **not** in the text on page 70.

   a) Water that falls from the sky…………………….

   b) The part of your body that controls everything…………………….

   c) A way of writing to a person on a computer…………………….

   d) A man who serves food in a restaurant …………………………

   e) Something you put on your walls with a brush to change the colour …………………

   f) A European country near Portugal and France ……………………

2 Write as many words as you can with three letters (one consonant + ay)

e.g. day

Write as many words as you can with four letters (two consonants + ay)

e.g. stay

3 Listen and fill the gaps in the conversation   🎧 **18.6**

Can you give me some information about ……………to Birmingham………………?

Are you coming back…………….?

Yes, what's the cheapest ……………to travel?

A cheap …………return is best, but you have to ……………until 10.15. That's the first …………after 9.30.

That's fine.

Do you have a…………………….?

No. How do I get one?

Are you aged between 16 and 25?

Yes, I'm 22.

Then you fill in this form and ……….for the railcard. After that you ……….money on your journey …………and all the off-peak journeys you ……………this year.

How much is it?

4 Listen again to 18.1 and write the words you hear.   🎧 **18.1**

Write

Find and practise filling in an online form to buy tickets or to buy a railcard, but stop before they can take your money!

Learn how to learn

Work with the spell-check

A computer spell-check can be very useful. When you type in a word-processing program, the computer can underline misspellings. It can also suggest correct spellings.

1   Read this text, which somebody typed in a word-processing   programme. There is one spelling mistake. Can you find it?

> Yesterday I went by train to Leeds to do some shopping. I caght the early morning train and I arrived at the shops before 10 o'clock.

If you click on the spell-check (usually 'tools' then 'spelling'), the computer will show you something like this:

Not in dictionary
Caght the early morning train and I arrived at the shops before 10 o'clock
Suggestions
Caught

If you click on the correct spelling (the word '**caught**', shown here in blue), the computer will automatically put it in place of the word you spelled wrong.

2   However, you need to make sure the computer doesn't do all the work if you want to improve your own spelling.

So, don't click on the word '**caught**' immediately. Look at the word and notice the spelling. Type it again, then click on the spell-check again to see if you got it right.

3   You can use the computer spell-check to test yourself.

Usually, the computer automatically checks spelling as you type.

If you want to test yourself, switch off the spell-check and type. When you have finished, switch the spell-check on again. See whether you have any mistakes.

UNIT 19
Sightseeing

'igh'

 Please refer to tracks 69–71 on the audio CD for this unit.

Rani is visiting her cousins in Canada and is writing a blog, so that her family and friends can read what she is doing. Read this extract from her blog.

Thursday
Arrived on time, but exhausted. The flight was good, no delays, but night flights are always tiring. Nearly all the family came to meet me at the airport – it was great – lots to talk about. They all send their love to everybody in the UK.

Friday
Spent time resting, while most of the family are at work. I sat in the garden most of the day. The weather is good – really bright sunshine this afternoon.

Monday
Yesterday we went sight-seeing. This place is beautiful! We went to a small town in the mountains, and the weather was just right – not too hot, not too cold. There's a cable car that goes up one of the mountains, straight up the side of the mountain – rocks one side, nothing the other!!! Very scary, but impressive. We were really high up, with a fantastic view all around. The best thing was that we stayed there till after dark, and it was fascinating to see all the lights come on in the town below and in the distance too.

Going shopping now – will try not to spend too much.

Answer the questions below.

a) Did Rani fly in the daytime?

b) Who came to meet her at the airport?

c) What was the weather like on Friday afternoon?

d) Where did they go on Sunday?

e) How did they get to the top of the mountain?

f) How long did they stay there?

g) What could they see at the end of their time on the mountain?

Read and notice

Read blogs.

Find leaflets or Internet sites advertising tourist attractions in your town and read them.

Do you know any of them?

Which ones would you like to go to?

Think about the spelling

1   Find the words

Highlight all the words in the text on the facing page with the letter sequence 'igh'. There are eight different words.

2   Look and learn

a)   Draw around the '-ight' shape in these words:

bright

lights

in the night

b)   Look at the eight 'igh' words in the text on the facing page. Write them like this:

n igh t

Circle the letters 'igh, like this:

Notice: Which letter normally comes after 'igh'?

Which word does not have this letter?

c)   Read these words and sentences below.

straight   Go <u>straight</u> ahead and you will see the taxi rank.

eight   The plane leaves at <u>eight</u> o'clock.

weight   Check the <u>weight</u> of your baggage. You have to pay more if it is over 20 kilograms.

With these three words, there is a vowel letter before 'igh'. Write the three words with this letter in a different colour:

straight

3   Listen and learn

1.   Listen to some words with 'igh' spelling. They all have the same vowel sound. It is the same sound as in words like 'time', 'find' and 'cry'.   🎧 **19.1**

2.   Listen to these words: straight, eight, weight.   🎧 **19.2**

These words have a vowel letter before 'igh'. Notice that the vowel sound is different from the vowel sound in the first group of words.

Be careful

Sometimes different countries have different spelling, e.g.

British English: tonight
American English: tonite

Practise the spelling

1 Put the right words in the gaps. You can listen as you write, or after you finish 🎧 **19.3**
writing. All the words have the letter sequence 'igh' in them.

a) Go .... ahead for about 100 metres, then turn left and take the first turning on the
....

b) Is it OK if I turn the .... on? It's very dark in here.

c) I'm working the day shift this week, but next week I'm on the .... shift.

d) Welcome to .... number 2987 to New York. This is your captain speaking.

e) There was a big .... between two gangs in the street. We had to call the police.

f) Does the jacket fit you well?

   No, it's too .... I need a bigger size.

g) Would you like another cake?

   No, thanks. I'm trying to lose ....

2 Look at these pairs of words below. The pronunciation is exactly the same, but the spelling and
the meaning are different. Put the correct words in the gaps. Use a dictionary if you need to.

a) right / write   Can you .... it down for me?

                        First turn left, then turn ....

                        I .... with my .... hand.

b) sight / site   It was a beautiful ....

                        He works on a building ....

c) higher / hire   I don't want to buy the tools for the job. I want to .... them

                        These mountains are .... than the mountains in my
                        country.

3 Listen again to Audio 19.1 and write the words you hear. 🎧 **19.1**

Write

Write your own blog.

Write about what you did this week, or write about a place you visited recently.

Learn how to learn

Be careful with spell-check

When you use a word-processing program, the computer can underline spelling mistakes. It can also change the spelling to a correct spelling. But there can be problems with this.

Look at the examples of the spell-check responding to someone trying to spell the word 'journey'.

Correct spelling: JOURNEY

A

Not in dictionary
juorney
Suggestions
journey
journeys

B

Not in dictionary
jurny
Suggestions
jury
journey
journeys

C

Not in dictionary
gerny
Suggestions
gurney
grey
germ

Student A made a small mistake and the computer found the right word.

Student B made a bigger mistake. The computer found the right word, but it was not the first choice.

Student C made a big mistake and the computer could not find the right word.

How do you know if the computer has the right word?

If you are not sure, use a dictionary to check the meaning of the word the computer gives you.

Road signs

vowel sounds with 'oa' and 'ow'

 Please refer to tracks 72–76 on the audio CD for this unit.

Read the road signs below.

1

ROAD AHEAD CLOSED

2
LOW BRIDGE AHEAD

3
Follow diversion signs

4
BOAT SHOW 12 miles

5

Go slow Road works AHEAD

6
Shallow water NO boating

7
NARROW ROAD

Think about the meaning

1 Look at these four road signs without words. Write the meaning in words under each one (all of them are at the top of the page).

2 Find words in the signs which mean the opposite of the words below.

a) Fast – ....

b) Wide – ....

c) High – ....

d) Deep – ....

Read and notice

Read the signs you see around you.

Download a copy of 'The Highway Code' and read the signs and their meanings.

Think about the spelling

1 Find the words

Look at the road signs on the facing page. Underline all the words with 'oa' and 'ow'.

2 Look and learn

a) Write the 'oa' words with the 'oa' in large letters and highlight them.

r oad

Write the 'ow' words with the 'ow' in large letters and highlight them.

Notice: When do you normally write 'oa' and when do you normally write 'ow'?

b) Write the name of these things in the table below. They all have 'oa' in them.

goal					

c) Read the words below and write them in the table according to the spelling.

road	low	boat	show	slow	soap	coat
so	goal	go	grow	toast	no	snow	know

Words with 'oa'	Words with 'ow'	Words with 'o'

3 Listen and learn   🎧 **20.1**

a) Listen to somebody reading the road signs out loud, and notice these words:
road; closed; low; follow; boat; show; go; slow; shallow; narrow

b) Listen to the list of words in the table in **2c**) above. They all have the same   🎧 **20.2**
vowel sound, but there are three different spelling patterns.

c) Read and listen to the words below. They have the 'o' + silent 'e' spelling (see   🎧 **20.3**
Unit 10), but they have exactly the same vowel sound as the 'oa' and 'ow' words:

closed; phone; home

Be careful

'ow' comes at the end of the word very often, but not always, e.g. 'bowl' – 'we gave the cat a bowl
of milk'.

'ow' is a common spelling for the sound in 'slow' and 'grow', but it is also a common   🎧 **20.4**
spelling for the sound in 'now' and 'how'. Listen and notice the pronunciation:
(1) slow; grow (2) now; how

Practise the spelling

1 Write the words on the crossword. All the words have the spelling 'oa' or 'ow'.

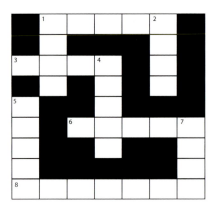

Across

1 My son scored two .... for his school football team.

3 He doesn't like flying, so he's travelling by .... and train.

6 The .... can be very dangerous in bad weather, when some drivers are not careful.

8 If you can't swim, you must stay in the .... end of the swimming pool.

Down

1 I give my children lots of fruit, because I want them to .... up healthy.

2 We need to buy .... powder for the washing machine.

4 Don't .... paper away. Recycle it.

5 Both my daughters need new .... for the winter.

7 This train is very .... It takes one hour longer than the next train.

2 Which is the right word?   🎧 **20.5**

Listen to these sentences in Audio 20.5. There are two words that sound exactly the same, but have different spelling patterns. Write the correct word in each sentence.

a) *Know or no?*

Is it cold outside? ...., it isn't.

Is it cold outside? I don't ....

b) *Knows or nose?*

My .... is cold.

He .... it's cold.

3 Listen again to Audio 20.2 and write the words you hear.   🎧 **20.2**

Write

Write signs and notices to help people find their way around a town or a building.

Learn how to learn

Keep a personal spelling book

It is a good idea to keep a personal spelling book, where you write the words you need to spell

You can do this in different ways:

- You can write words <u>after</u> you have learned them.
- You can write words <u>before</u> you learn them, and look at them again and again.

You can organise the words in different ways:

- You can write them alphabetically, with one page for each letter of the alphabet.
- You can put words together with the same spelling pattern.
- You can put words together with similar meaning.

You can do it electronically or on paper:

- You can keep a notebook and carry it around with you.
- You can organise a computer file with your words.

Think about what you want to do

I want to learn the words first, then put them in my spelling book, so I don't forget them	
I want to put the words in my spelling book before I learn them, and look at them again and again	
I want to organise the words alphabetically	
I want to put words together with the same spelling pattern	
I want to put words together with a similar meaning	
I want to keep a paper-based notebook	
I want to use a computer for keeping my words together	

UNIT 21
A personal account

plurals

 Please refer to track 77 on the audio CD for this unit.

Read Jane's account about her home, her work and her family.

My name is Jane and I live with my family. I am married with two teenage children and one baby! Before my baby was born, I worked part time in an office, but now I work for the same company from my own home. I have a photocopier, fax machine and of course the Internet, so I can keep in touch with my boss. She sends emails and faxes for me to deal with, so I don't need to go to the office much. I go to a computer class once a week. There is a day nursery at the college, so my baby goes there. Last year I also went to English classes for two days a week, but not this year.

My husband works in an electrical goods factory. He has a very long journey to work, so he leaves early and comes back late. Luckily, his company is moving to the city centre. This is good, because we live near the city centre. As for me, I have no journeys to work!

I have two sisters, Diana and Emma, but they don't live near me. In fact, the three of us all live in different cities: me in Leeds, Diana in Bristol and Emma in London. My sister Diana lives near the countryside, but Emma lives in an industrial area. There are a lot of factories near where she lives.

Both my sisters are married. Emma and her husband work for computer companies, but not the same one. Diana's husband has a job in a library. My sister Diana works two days a week as a childminder. She looks after two babies, but she's also studying part time to be a nursery teacher. There are some good nurseries where she lives. There is also a large family centre, where they look after children for working families, so I think there are good job opportunities for Diana.

Think about the meaning

Fill in the chart below with information about Jane's family.

	Jane	Diana's husband	Emma
Where they live – the city – the area		Bristol Near the countryside	
Where they work			

Read and notice

Read personal accounts in magazines.

Think about the spelling

1 **Find the words**

   a) Read paragraphs one and two of the text on the facing page.

      Highlight the words below:

      | family | city | journey | day | nursery | factory |
      | company | baby | fax | class | | |

   b) Read the rest of the text.

      Find the plurals of the same words and highlight them in a different colour. The plurals may be in any part of the text.

2 **Look and learn**

   a) Add the plural words to the table below.

Singular	Plural
family city nursery factory company baby	
journey day	

   Notice: Why are 'journey' and 'day' in a different box?

   Why is the plural different from the other words?

   b) Write 'family' then cross out the 'y' and add 'ies'.

   family̶ + ies

   Take some small pieces of paper and a pair of scissors. Write 'family' on one piece of paper, write 'ies' on the other, then physically cut off the 'y' from family before you join it to the 'ies'. Do the same with the other words.

   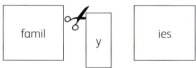

   c) Write the plural of these words below. They are all regular plurals.

      book   table   chair   cake   banana   cup   dog   biscuit   light

      Write the plural of these two words (they are in the text on the facing page):

      fax   class

      How is the plural different from the regular plurals.

      Why do you think it is different?

3 **Listen and learn**

   Listen to the list of plural words. All the words end in 's', but sometimes you hear an 's' sound and sometimes a 'z' sound.

    21.1

Be careful

Many common words do not add 's' in the plural, e.g.

man – men; woman – women; child – children

Practise the spelling

1 Write the plural of these words:

a) Key   ....

b) Library   ....

c) Cross   ....

d) Box   ....

e) Lady   ....

f) Boy   ....

g) Tax   ....

h) Dress   ....

i) Copy   ....

2 Change these sentences to the plural.

Don't forget you sometimes need to change the verb.

a) Put the book in the bag.

b) Put the dress in the box.

c) Who is the lady over there? (Change 'is' to 'are')

d) We saw a football match. (Change 'a' to 'two')

e) Can I make a photocopy? (Change 'a' to 'some)

f) They have a baby. (Change 'a' to 'two')

g) We bought a watch. (Change 'a' to 'some')

h) We went to the zoo and saw a monkey. (Change 'a' to 'some')

3 Listen again to Audio 21.1 and write the words you hear.   🎧 **21.1**

Write

Write an account of your life, your family and your work.

Learn how to learn

Learn common endings

When you use a dictionary, you pay attention to the beginnings of words.
But many words in English have common endings. If you can spell these endings, it can help you to spell lots of words.

1 Look at this common ending 'er'.

Read the text for Unit 21 'A personal account'

Find five words which end in 'er'.

....

....

....

....

....

2 Here are some more common endings:

......ive.

.....able.

..... tion.

Read the text for Unit 19 'Sightseeing' and find one word ending in ' ...ive'.

Read the text for Unit 12 'Driving lessons' and find another word ending in '...ive'.

Read the text for Unit 14 'A holiday' and find one word ending in '...able'.

Read the text for Unit 15 'Supermarket shopping' and find another word ending in '...able'.

Read the text for Unit 13 'In the town' and find one word ending in '...tion'.

Read the text for Unit 17 'The local council' and find another word ending in '...tion'.

Write these words and try and think of other words with the same endings.

A traditional story

'ed' endings

 Please refer to tracks 78–79 on the audio CD for this unit.

Read the story below.

The man, the boy and the donkey

Once there was a man who wanted to sell his donkey, so he decided to take the donkey to the market with his young son.

The man, the boy and the donkey started to walk along the path towards the market. Suddenly, some people stopped them and asked the man why he did not ride on the donkey. The man wanted to please the people, so he climbed up on the donkey's back.

After a while, they met some other people, who shouted: "You lazy man. You ride on the donkey, while the boy walks". The man got down and the boy got on the donkey.

Soon, some other people stopped them and said the boy was lazy to sit on the donkey while the man walked. This time, the man and the boy both sat on the donkey together.

This did not please the next people. They said: "The poor donkey. You both sit on the donkey and you don't care how the donkey feels". So in the end, the man and the boy grabbed the donkey, lifted it and carried it down the road towards the market.

The next people laughed and laughed when they saw them. They laughed until they cried. So the man and the boy put the donkey down, walked beside the donkey and, with their heads down, they hurried to the market.

They tried to please everybody, but they pleased nobody.

Think about the meaning

Put these events in the order they happened in the story.

a) The man sat on the donkey.

b) The man and boy walked with the donkey.

c) The man and boy both sat on the donkey.

d) The man and boy carried the donkey.

e) The boy sat on the donkey.

What is the moral of the story?

Read and notice

Read other stories. Look in your library for interesting stories.

Think about the spelling

1 **Find the words**

a) Read the text on the facing page and find the past tenses of the verbs below. Write the past tense next to the base form.

Base form	Past tense		Base form	Past tense
walk laugh want start shout climb			stop grab cry carry hurry try	

b) **Notice**: What happens with these words: stop; grab?
What happens with these words: cry; carry; hurry; try?

2 **Look and learn**

a) Look at the base form of these verbs. They all have 'ed' in the past tense:
want; carry; stop; copy; plan; fry; start; finish; jog; talk; marry; fit

Take 12 small pieces of paper and write one of the verbs on each piece.

want   carry   stop

Sort the papers into three groups: words where you double letters; words where you change 'y' to 'ied'; words where you only add 'ed'.

b) Write the past tense of the verbs in the table below.

Add 'ed'	Double consonant + 'ed'	Change 'y' to 'i' + 'ed'

3 **Listen and learn**   **22.1**

Listen to some verbs in the base form and past tense. They all have 'ed' in the spelling of the past tense, but they don't all have the same sound at the end.

Which ones have a 't' sound at the end in the past tense?

In which ones do you hear the vowel sound in the 'ed' ending?

Be careful

Some verbs have 'd' at the end, but not 'ed', such as:

say – said
pay – paid

Practise the spelling

1 Listen to Audio 22.2 and fill the gaps below.   🎧 **22.2**

They .... to walk along the path towards the market.

Some people .... them.

The man .... to please the people.

The man and the boy .... the donkey, ... it and .... it down the road towards the market.

The next people laughed until they ....

So the man and the boy put the donkey down, ...beside the donkey, and with their heads down, they .... to the market.

2 Read the sentences below and change the underlined verbs to the past tense.

a) I <u>stop</u> the car at the traffic lights.

b) I <u>carry</u> my books in my bag.

c) They <u>jog</u> in the park in the morning.

d) We always <u>photocopy</u> our work.

e) When they <u>cook</u>, they always <u>fry</u> the potatoes.

f) I always <u>try</u> to help them.

3 'ed' endings are not only for past tense, e.g.

'Do you sell canned drinks?'

'No, only cartons'

Read the verbs, then write a word with an 'ed' ending, to fill the gaps:

fit; tin; marry

a) My sister is getting ....next month.

b) I want fresh tomatoes, not ....tomatoes.

c) I would like to have a ....carpet in my room.

Write

Write the story of the man, the boy and the donkey in your own words.

Write in your own words another traditional story that you know.

Learn how to learn

Check your learning

Check the spelling patterns you have learned.

Write a few words with the same spelling pattern in each box below:

Clean Cream Meat Please		

What else have you learned since you started working with this book?

....

....

....

....

....

What methods do you like to use to help you remember spellings?

....

....

....

....

....

Answers

Unit 1 Shopping lists

Page 2

Think about the meaning

1 Who sent the letter from the school?
The head teacher (J. Ahmed)

Why does Sara need to buy clothes for her son?
He needs clothes for sports day

When is the school sports day?
Friday, 17th April

Page 3

Think about the spelling

1 **Find the words**

Sara is going shopping. She needs to buy clothes for her son as well as food.

```
Dear Parent

As you may know, we have our school
sports day next Friday, the 17th of
April.

Your child needs to bring:
A pair of shorts
A T-shirt (with short sleeves)
A pair of trainers or running shoes

If you wish to come to the sports
day, you will be welcome. We start
at 1.30 p.m.

Yours sincerely


J. Ahmed (head teacher)
```

Shopping list
Chicken legs
Fish
Tea bags
Milk
Cheddar cheese
Butter
Bread
Ice cream
Chocolate sauce

Who sent the letter from the school?
Why does Sara need to buy clothes for her son?
When is the school sports day?

Where do you go to buy clothes?
Which shop do you go to for food?

2 **Look and learn**

a) sh   ch

   shopping   child
   shorts   chicken
   shirt   cheddar
   short   cheese
   shoes   chocolate
   shop

3 **Listen and learn**

b) shopping, shoes, shirt, shorts
   child, chicken, cheese, chocolate

c) a   2 chips
    b   1 ships
    c   1 ships
    d   2 chips
    e   2 chips
    f   1 ships

Page 4

Practise the spelling

1 sh   ch

   ship   children
   fish   chips
   she   change
   shop   chest
   shoes   chair
   shoulder   cheap
   shy   champion
   English

2 a) English people love fish and chips.
     b) My children need new shoes.
     c) The big shops are expensive, but the market is cheap.
     d) We bought a table and four new chairs.
     e) Her daughter doesn't speak much – she's a very shy girl.
     f) Can you change a £20 note?
     g) I had an accident and hurt my shoulder and my chest.
     h) Who will win the football championship this year?

3 a) When did you arrive here?

b) Who is your teacher?

c) What do you want?

d) Where do you live?

e) How many children have you got?

f) Why do you want this job?

Page 5

Learn how to learn

Consonants and vowels

1 The alphabet

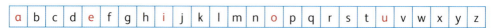

a b c d e f g h i j k l m n o p q r s t u v w x y z

2 Consonants

Same sound, but different letters – 'gentle' and 'jam'

Same letters, but two different sounds – 'gentle' and 'going'

Two letters make one sound – 'this', 'thing', 'what', 'shoe', 'chair', 'sing'

Unit 2 Birthdays

Page 6

Think about the meaning

1

Monday	Tuesday	Wednesday	Thursday	Friday	Saturday	Sunday
	1	2	3	Krystyna's birthday 4	5	6
7	8	9	10	11	12	13
14	15	16	Adam's birthday 17	18	Party 19	20
21	22	23	24	25	26	Teresa's birthday 27
28	29	30	31			

2 Examples:

Tuesday the 1st of October

Wednesday the 2nd of October

Thursday the 3rd of October

Friday the 4th of October

Saturday the 5th of October

Page 7

Think about the spelling

1 Find the words

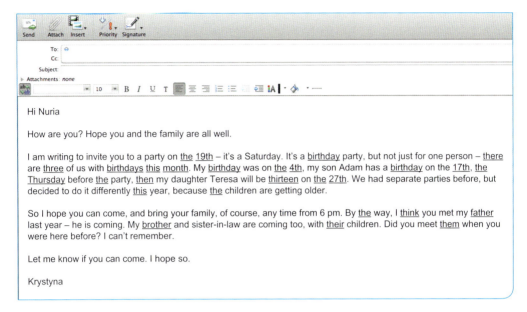

Hi Nuria

How are you? Hope you and the family are all well.

I am writing to invite you to a party on <u>the</u> <u>19th</u> – it's a Saturday. It's a <u>birthday</u> party, but not just for one person – <u>there</u> are <u>three</u> of us with <u>birthdays</u> <u>this</u> <u>month</u>. My <u>birthday</u> was on <u>the</u> <u>4th</u>, my son Adam has a <u>birthday</u> on the <u>17th</u>, <u>the</u> <u>Thursday</u> before <u>the</u> party, <u>then</u> my daughter Teresa will be <u>thirteen</u> on <u>the</u> <u>27th</u>. We had separate parties before, but decided to do it differently <u>this</u> year, because <u>the</u> children are getting older.

So I hope you can come, and bring your family, of course, any time from 6 pm. By <u>the</u> way, I <u>think</u> you met my <u>father</u> last year – he is coming. My <u>brother</u> and sister-in-law are coming too, with <u>their</u> children. Did you meet <u>them</u> when you were here before? I can't remember.

Let me know if you can come. I hope so.

Krystyna

Page 8

Practise the spelling

1 This is a picture of my son's wedding.

That young woman is my daughter.

These people are my relatives.

Those people are friends.

My son had a big wedding.

There were about 50 people at the ceremony in the mosque and more than 200 at the party.

2 a) My mother and father live in India.

b) If the weather is nice, we can sit in the park.

c) Would you like another cup of tea?

d) If you want to go swimming, we can go together.

e) I have two sisters and one brother.

Unit 3 College

Page 10

Think about the meaning

1 What do people learn in a catering college?
They learn about cooking, restaurant work and hotel work.

2 Are the sentences true or false?

The college is south of the city centre.	False
The 301 bus stops outside the college.	True
The buses go from Queen Street bus station.	False
There are separate canteens for students and staff.	True
The library is next to the key skills department.	False
Classrooms 11–19 are upstairs.	True

Page 11

Think about the spelling

1 Find the words

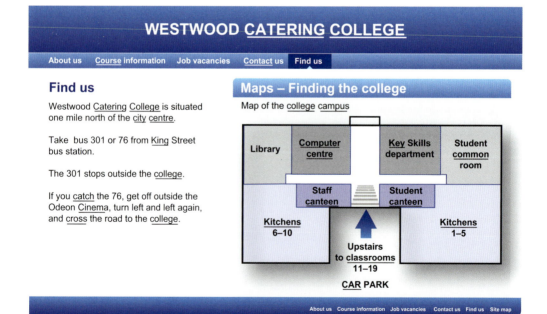

2 Look and learn

a) What is the second letter?

a	e	i	o	u
(c)anteen catering car	(Ke)y Keyboard kettle	(ki)tchens king	(co)llege computer coffee	(cu)p

b) 'c' comes before 'a', 'o' and 'u'. 'k' comes before 'e' and 'i'.

3 Listen and learn

a)

Begins with 'k'	Begins with 'c' 'c' sounds like 'k' in 'king'	Begins with 'c' 'c' sounds like 's' in 'sing'	Begins with 'c' Another consonant follows
king key kitchens kettle keyboard	college campus catering catch canteen computer common car cup coffee course contact	city cinema centre	cross classrooms
Which two vowels can follow 'k'? 'e' and 'i'	Which three vowels can follow 'c'? 'a', 'o' and 'u'	Which two vowels can follow 'c'? 'e' and 'i'	

b) When does 'c' sounds like 'k' in king?
Before 'a', 'o' and 'u' or before another consonant ('r' or 'l').

When does 'c' sound like 's' in sing?
Before 'e' and 'I'.

Page 12

Practise the spelling

1 Where can you find cars?   In the car park
Where can you find a kettle?   In the kitchen
Where can you find a keyboard?   In the computer centre
Where can you find cups of coffee?   In the canteen

2 Write 'c' or 'k' in the gaps
  a) Would you like a cup of coffee?
  b) I lost my key and had to call my husband at work.
  c) Can you help me in the kitchen?
  d) I need to buy a new keyboard for my computer.
  e) Can I help you? Thank you, that's very kind of you?
  f) Our cat had six kittens.

3 Ladies and <u>G</u>entlemen (soft)
  <u>G</u>et off the bus at the bus station (hard)
  Can you <u>g</u>ive me a hand? (hard)
  Their house has a lovely <u>g</u>arden (hard)
  He speaks French and <u>G</u>erman (soft)
  She's secretary to the <u>G</u>eneral Mana<u>g</u>er (soft; soft)

Page 13

Capital letters

1 Monday
  Tuesday
  Wednesday
  Thursday
  Friday
  Saturday
  Sunday

  January
  February
  March
  April
  May
  June
  July
  August
  September
  October
  November
  December

3 River Thames and Manchester Road are names of a particular river and a particular road. In the other sentences, 'river' and 'road' are not names.

4 a) The President of the United States lives in the White House.
   b) My uncle has a nice house.
   c) I live in a noisy street.
   d) My address is 40 High Street.
   e) Cairo is a city on the River Nile.
   f) I like to walk by the river in the evening.
   g) This is a very old building.

5 Change letters to capitals where necessary.

I like London. I have a flat near Hammersmith Bridge. When I want to go anywhere, I get the train from Hammersmith Station. I like to go to Oxford Street, as there are some good shops there, for example Selfridges. I often go there on a Saturday. Sometimes, I like to walk in Hyde Park. There is a park near my home, but it's quite small.

Unit 4 Fitness

Page 14

Think about the meaning

1 Who thinks it's good to eat low fat food?   Shiv
2 Who thinks golf is fun?   Ben
3 Who jogs in the park every morning?   Lam
4 Who swims three times a week?   Anna
5 Who thinks push-ups can help?   Tom
6 Who thinks it's a good idea to walk to the next bus stop?   Sam
7 Who runs in the park every Sunday?   Abdul

Page 15

Think about the spelling

1 **Find the words**

Matt:	I am totally un<u>fit</u>! I need to <u>get fit</u> before I start my new <u>job</u>. <u>Help</u>! How do I do it? Any ideas?
Comment – Anna:	Do what I do. I <u>swim</u> three times a week.
Comment – Tom:	Do <u>ten push-ups</u> every morning – that works!
Comment – Abdul:	Do the same as me – go for a <u>run</u> in the park every Sunday.
Comment – Lam:	I <u>jog</u> in the park every morning – come with me next time.
Comment – Ben:	Play <u>golf</u> – it's exercise and it's <u>fun</u>.
Comment – Sam:	Don't be lazy. Don't <u>get</u> the <u>bus</u> to work – walk! If not the whole way, walk to the next <u>bus stop.</u>

Comment – Shiv: I put lots of weight on last year, but I'm OK now. Eat low-fat food, and if you get hungry between meals, don't eat, drink some water instead.

2 Look and learn

a	e	i	o	u
fat	help	fit	job	up
back	get	swim	jog	push
hand	ten	drink	lots	bus
	leg	hip	stop	run
	neck		golf	fun
	left			put

Notice: All words have only one vowel letter. Some have only one consonant letter at the end of the word, but some have two.

3 Listen and learn

b) Number 1 – pin
Number 2 – pen
Number 3 – cup
Number 4 – cap
Number 5 – men
Number 6 – man
Number 7 – pot
Number 8 – put

Page 16

Practise the spelling

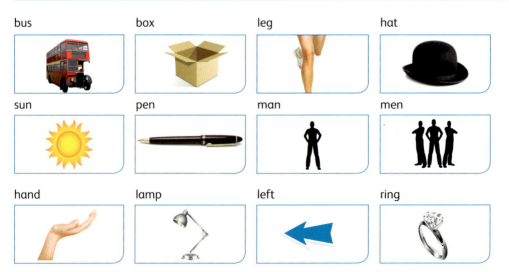

bus	box	leg	hat
sun	pen	man	men
hand	lamp	left	ring

Unit 5 Clothes

Page 18

Think about the meaning

1	What are the colours available for jeans?	Blue and black.
2	Where are the pockets on the jeans?	Front and back.
3	Are the socks for hot or cold weather?	Cold weather.
4	How many pairs of socks can you get for £7.99?	Six pairs.
5	What size of jackets can you buy?	Sizes 10–16.
6	How much do you pay for postage and packing if you order now?	Nothing.

Page 19

1 Find the words

pockets; back; black; thick; socks; pack; jackets; packing

2

a			e			i			o			u		
bl	ack		ch	eck		th	ick		p	ock	et	l	uck	y
j	ack	et	n	eck		ch	ick	en	s	ock	s	tr	uck	
p	ack					s	ick		cl	ock				
b	ack					qu	ick	ly						
p	ack	ing												

3 Listen and learn

iii) 1 track (sentence a)

2 truck (sentence b)

3 luck (sentence d)

4 lock (sentence c)

5 check (sentence f)

6 chick (sentence e)

Page 20

Practise the spelling

1 a) Can you lock the door when you leave? (luck / lock)

b) Good luck with your exam. (luck / lock)

c) My brother drives a truck. (truck / track)

d) This is my favourite track on this CD. (truck / track)

e) I bought a packet of biscuits. (packet / pocket)

f) There's a hole in my coat pocket. (packet / pocket)

g) What time is it? 6 o' clock. (click / clock)

h) To reach the website, click on the link. (click / clock)

2 Nick was a truck driver. He had to travel from England to France and back three times a week and he sometimes got very tired.

This morning he had to get up at 5 o'clock to start work. The alarm went off and he woke, but went back to sleep, then woke up again suddenly at 5.30.

He jumped out of bed and ran downstairs. He grabbed his jacket but a packet of cigarettes fell out of the pocket. When he bent down to pick it up, he moved too quickly and hurt his back and his neck so badly that he felt sick.

In the end, he just went back to bed and forgot about work until the next day.

Unit 6 Jobs

Page 22

a) Yusuf is a taxi driver now	False
b) Yusuf's daughter wants to be a teacher	True
c) Yusuf's older son wants to be an actor	False
d) Anna works full time as a cleaner	False
e) Anna likes her job	False
f) Anna would like to be a hairdresser	True
g) Samira's manager speaks Arabic	False
h) Samira has a solicitor	True
i) Samira wants to be independent	True

Page 23

Think about the spelling

1

> **Yusuf's story**
>
> In my country, I was a taxi <u>driver</u>, but now I am a <u>waiter</u> in a Turkish restaurant. I have three children, all at school. My daughter wants to be a <u>teacher</u>, and my older son wants to be a <u>lawyer</u>. My other son says he wants to be an <u>actor</u> or a <u>singer</u>, but I don't like that idea.

> **Anna's story**
>
> I have a part-time job as a <u>cleaner</u>, but I don't like it. It's hard work and I don't meet many people.
>
> I want to start college in September, because I would like to have a different job in the future. I would like to be a <u>hairdresser</u>.

> **Samira's story**
>
> I speak Arabic, but I'm learning English, because I need it in my daily life. A lot of people at my work speak Arabic, but the <u>manager</u> and the <u>supervisor</u> speak only English.
>
> When I go to the <u>doctor</u> or to my <u>solicitor</u>, my friend comes with me to help with English, but I want to be independent and do things for myself.

2 Look and learn

b)

Words ending in 'er'	Words ending in 'or'
driv**er**	act**or**
wait**er**	supervis**or**
teach**er**	doct**or**
lawy**er**	solicit**or**
sing**er**	
clean**er**	
hairdress**er**	
manag**er**	

c)

doctor	driver	actor	cleaner
solicitor	waiter	dancer	footballer

d) daughter
   older
   September

Page 24

Practise the spelling

1 My son wants to be a doctor.

My father is a bus driver.

My brother and my sister are solicitors.

Footballers earn lots of money.

I worked as a lawyer before I came to the UK.

3

¹S	I	S	T	E	R					
²A	C	T	O	R						
	³C	L	E	A	N	E	R			
⁴W	A	I	T	E	R					
⁵D	O	C	T	O	R					
⁶D	R	I	V	E	R					
⁷F	A	T	H	E	R					
⁸F	O	O	T	B	A	L	L	E	R	
⁹H	A	I	R	D	R	E	S	S	E	R

Unit 7 Hotel work

Page 26

Think about the meaning

1 Where can you expect to see the notices?
In a newspaper; on a form; in a kitchen; on the menu; outside the restaurant

a) in a newspaper

b) on the menu

c) on a form

d) outside the restaurant

e) on the menu

f) in a kitchen

2 Write a word that means:

a) People who work in a place ......staff.......

b) Mineral water without gas ......still...........

c) It tells you how much you have to pay...bill........

Page 27

1

2 Look and learn

a)

What are the consonants at the end?				
ss	ll	nn	zz	ff
address	full	inn	jazz	staff
waitress	grill			
glass	bill			
miss	still			

b) One vowel letter comes before the double consonants.

c)

Page 28

Practise the spelling

1 a) I go to an English class two days a week.

b) "Do you sell Chinese noodles?" "I'm sorry, we don't."

c) I miss my old home.

d) I don't know where I can find the money to pay this bill.

e) "Can I go home? I don't feel very well."

f) Don't push the door. Pull it.

g) It's difficult to work if your boss is unfriendly.

h) The favourite game in my family is chess.

2 Circle the last three letters of all the words below.

class	kill	sell	full	grass	chess	cross
miss	kiss	bill	pull	address	boss	well

3 Rhymes
Examples:

grass	class, glass, pass
kill	bill, fill, mill
well	sell, bell, tell

Unit 8 Comparing people and places

Page 30

Think about the meaning

Which sister is shorter, the older or the younger?	The younger
Which sister is slimmer, the older or the younger?	The older
Which town is bigger, in Africa or in England?	In England
Which place is hotter, Africa or England?	Africa
When is the African town wetter than the town in England?	In the rainy season

Page 31

1 **Find the words**

a)

Comparing people

 I am one of three sisters, and we all look different. My <u>older</u> sister is very tall. I am a bit <u>shorter</u> than her and my <u>younger</u> sister is very short.

I think that my sisters are slim, but the <u>younger</u> one thinks she is too fat. She always says she is <u>fatter</u> than me, but I don't think she is. My <u>older</u> sister is certainly <u>slimmer</u> than me. She is the slimmest person in the family.

Comparing places

 I was born in a small town in Central Africa, but now I live in England. The places are very different. My town in England is much <u>bigger</u> than my town in Africa, and there are more things to buy and things to do, but I am not sure that life here is <mark>better</mark>.

The weather is also different. Of course, Africa is <u>hotter</u> than England, but I like the English weather sometimes. It can be hot in July or August, but it is not usually too hot. Sometimes England can be very wet, for example in March or April, but in the rainy season in my country, it can be even <u>wetter</u> than in England.

---

b) The comparative of 'good' is 'better' – highlighted in yellow above.

2 **Look and learn**

a) young……...younger ……..   hot …………hotter……………………....

short………shorter………..   slim…………slimmer………………......

old…………older………..   fat……………fatter………………………....

wet …………wetter………………………

big …………bigger………………………..

Notice: At the end of the words 'hot', 'slim', 'fat', 'wet' and 'big', there is one vowel letter and one consonant letter. The consonant doubles if there is one vowel letter and one consonant letter at the end

b)

	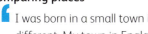			
Adjective	thin	cold	fit	fast
Comparative	thinner	colder	fitter	faster

c)

+ 'ing'	double the last consonant + 'ing'
work – work**ing**	run – ru**nning**
send – send**ing**	swim – swi**mming**
meet – meet**ing**	sit – si**tting**
jump – jump**ing**	cut – cu**tting**
rain – rain**ing**	jog – jo**gging**
	begin – begi**nning**

Page 32

Practise the spelling

1 a) I sit in my garden every morning.
        I like sitting in my garden.

   b) I jog one mile every day.
        I like jogging.

   c) I swim three times a week.
        I like swimming.

2

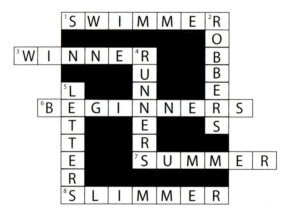

Unit 9 Money

Page 35

Think about the meaning

1 Which of the above notices could you find:

On a shop window	1
On a cash machine	3
On the website for an online shop	2
On a leaflet given out in the street	6
In a newspaper	4
On an online banking site	5

2 Match the word with the meaning

Cash	Money in the hand (paper money or coins)
Sale	A time when shops sell things more cheaply
Interest	If you borrow money, you pay back more; for example, 2% or 5%
Statement	The bank tells you (on paper or on the Internet) how much money you have in your account

Page 35

Think about the spelling

1 Find the words

1 END OF SEASON <u>SALE</u> 50% off many items	2 <u>Save</u> up to £100 on a new computer. Hurry, offer ends soon. Click **here** for details
3 Please <u>take</u> your cash	4 The Governor of the Bank of England said today that the interest <u>rate</u> will go up
5 Click **here** to see your current <u>statement</u> Click **here** to see your previous <u>statement</u>	6 <u>MAKE</u> MONEY IN YOUR FREE TIME EARN £££ WORKING FROM HOME

2 Look and learn

    b) name, same

        cake, make, take

        brave, save

        female, sale

        plate, late, rate

        race, place, face

Page 36

Practise the spelling

1 a) We watched a bicycle <u>race</u>.

    b) Your baby has a lovely <u>face</u>.

    c) <u>Take</u> care.

    d) Don't <u>make</u> a noise.

    e) Try not to <u>wake</u> the baby.

    f) He's looking for a <u>place</u> to live.

2

game	name
gate	late
place	face
make	cake
sale	pale
save	gave
age	page

3 a) My mother <u>gave</u> me some money for my birthday.

    b) He has a thin <u>face</u> and long, black hair.

    c) I started school at the <u>age</u> of six.

    d) Can you <u>make</u> sandwiches for the children's lunch?

    e) Please open the book at <u>page</u> 23.

    f) I love chocolate <u>cake</u>.

    g) I can't remember his <u>name</u>.

Page 37

Learn how to learn

Letter and sounds

1 Consonants

a) <u>pin</u> – bin

b) <u>best</u> – vest

c) fan – <u>van</u>

d) pan – <u>fan</u>

e) vest – <u>west</u>

f) nine – <u>line</u>

2 Vowels

a) <u>pan</u> – pen

b) pen – <u>pin</u>

c) <u>cat</u> – cut

d) boss – <u>bus</u>

Unit 10 Bank accounts

Page 38

Think about the meaning

1	What does she want to close?	Her old account
2	What does she want to open?	A new high rate account
3	What is her home phone number?	0113 356 9826
4	What is her postcode?	LS6 3DU
5	Does she have a mobile phone?	No

What is the past tense of these words?

phone: phoned

open: opened

close: closed

speak: spoke

Page 39

1 Find the words

"I phoned yesterday and spoke to somebody about my account. I want to close my old account and open a new high rate account. They said that's possible".

"Yes, it is. What's your account number?"

"50673421."

"And your name?"

"Jones. A Jones".

"And a couple of security questions – what's your date of birth?"

"29.6.75."

"And your mother's maiden name?"

"Morgan."

"Fine. I'll close your old account, then if you fill in this form, you can open your new account and transfer the money."

Now read the form that Anna filled in.

XYZ BANK – APPLICATION TO OPEN AN ACCOUNT	
Surname:	Jones
Other name:	Anna
Home address:	86 Hyde Park Lane
	Leeds
Postcode:	LS6 3DU
Phone:	0113 356 9826 (home)
	(work)
	(mobile)

3c The words 'post' and 'old' have two consonants at the end.

Page 40

Practise the spelling

1

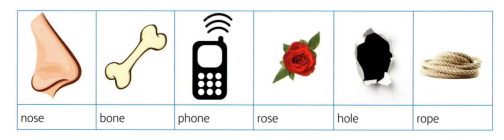

| nose | bone | phone | rose | hole | rope |

2 a) I arrived .....home........... very late last night.

   b) My friend lives ......alone.............. in a small flat.

   c) I lost some money because there is a ....hole......... in my pocket.

   d) My uncle is very funny. He tells lots of ....jokes............

   e) He had an accident and broke a .....bone....... in his foot.

   f) Roses..........are my favourite flowers.

3 Two of the words above have exactly the same pronunciation. Which ones are they?

   'hole' and 'whole'

   a) There was a .....hole.......... in the road and I fell over.

   b) My ......whole.......... family came to visit.

   c) My father lived his ....whole....... life in the same house.

   d) I lost my wallet because there was a .....hole....... in my pocket.

4 a) They speak Spanish   *They spoke Spanish*

   b) We break the record   *We broke the record*

   c) They steal things from their workplace   *They stole things from their workplace*

   d) I wake up early   *I woke up early*

   e) I ride my bike to work   *I rode my bike to work*

Page 41

Which words to learn?

1 Some common words are:
   name; with; friend; near; sometimes; one; like
   Words important for the student personally are: Poland; cashier; Liverpool

Unit 11 Restaurants

Page 42

Think about the meaning

1 Raj (vegetarian) can eat vegetable curry or cheese, onion and tomato pie.

   Sonia (doesn't like spicy food) can eat chicken supreme or cheese, onion and tomato pie. Both of them can eat fruit salad or apple pie.

Page 43

1 **Find the words**

Porter's Restaurant

Try our new lunchtime menu

2 courses for only £8.95

Chicken supreme

Chicken in a delicious white wine sauce,
with fine green beans and baby new potatoes

Spicy Chinese beef

Beef cooked with tomatoes and spices, with
stir-fry vegetables and noodles or rice

Vegetable curry

A vegetable curry with coconut (choose hot,
medium or mild), with mango chutney,
lime pickle and rice

Cheese, onion and tomato pie

A vegetarian dish made with fresh vegetables,
served with a side salad

❖❖❖❖

Exotic fruit salad

Fruit salad with mango and pineapple

Apple pie

A delicious apple pie, with cream or ice cream

The word 'pie' is different from the others because there is no consonant between the 'i' and the
'e'.

4 **Listen and learn**

1) b   rice

2) a   race

3) c   lake

4) d   like

5) f   mile

6) e   male

7) b   rice

8) c   lake

9) f   mile

10) a   race

Page 44

Practise the spelling

1 In Europe, many people drink wine with a meal. They usually drink red wine with red meat, such as beef, and white wine with white meat, such as chicken, or with fish. With vegetarian food, they sometimes drink red, sometimes white, as they like.

In Australia, people like to drink beer, ice cold, and in Japan there is a local wine made from rice.

Of course, many people never drink alcohol. If you travel in Asia, you can find very nice fruit cocktails, made from mango, pineapple, oranges or limes. Or why not try iced tea or coffee, when the weather is hot. It's delicious.

2 a) It belongs to me … mine ………….

b) A woman I am married to ……wife……….

c) A clock tells it to you ………time………..

d) Everything is OK ………fine…….

e) You open this when you want to use your computer…file…

f) More than one mouse ……………mice………..

g) This is just over two kilometres ………mile……….

h) A small green fruit, like a lemon ………lime………

i) The opposite of black………white………

Page 45

Learn how to learn

Split words into parts

2 To morr ow	some times	ex pen sive	com put er
to get her	co co nut	res taur ant	Sa tur day
diff er ent	ex amp le	ve get ar ian	to ma to

These are examples only. You may choose to split the words in a different way.

Unit 12 Driving lessons

Page 46

Think about the meaning

a) What is the name of the driving school?   The Harbour Driving School

b) How long do the driving courses last?   One week

c) When did Sabir Khan start driving lessons?   Three weeks ago

d) When is he taking his theory test?   On the 12th of July

e) When does he want to take his practical test?   In August

Page 47

1 **Find the words**

Are you <u>learning</u> to drive?
Or are you <u>thinking</u> about it?

- The Harbour <u>Driving</u> School   • Intensive <u>Driving</u> Courses
- Very high success rate   • Reasonable prices

Our intensive <u>driving</u> courses are each for one week, Monday to Friday.

Courses start every 2 weeks.

Book now!

Name:	*Sabir Khan*

Address: Postcode:	*35 Anderson Street, Portsmouth* *PO6 5JQ*

When would you like to start your course?

2nd July   (16th July)   30th July   13th August   27th August

Tell us something about your <u>driving</u> experience?

I had my first <u>driving</u> lesson three weeks ago. I had three lessons in June, and am going to have two more before your course begins. I am <u>taking</u> my theory test on the 12th of July, and I am <u>hoping</u> to take my practical test in August.

Base form	'ing' form
learn	learning
drive	driving
go	going
hope	hoping
take	taking
think	thinking

What happens to the words that end in 'e'.
The 'e' disappears when you add 'ing'.

Page 48

Practise the spelling

1 Read the first sentence and complete the others

   a) A person who drives is a driver.

   b) A person who writes is a writer.

   c) A person who bakes is a baker.

   d) A person who smokes is a smoker.

   e) A person who dances is a dancer.

2

driving	writing	hoping	making	taking
having	phoning	coming	closing	giving
shining	smiling	dancing	joking	shaving

3 a) They ………………are dancing…………..

   b) The sun ………is shining……………..

   c) He …………is driving ……………..

   d) He …is making the dinner………………………..

   e) She …………is phoning ………..her friend.

   f) He …is writing……………………

   g) She ………is closing………..the door.

   h) She ……is smiling…………….

Unit 13 In the town

Page 50

Think about the meaning

These are some examples:

The bank is next to the supermarket.

The department store is opposite the gardens.

The pharmacy is near the station.

Page 51

1 Find the words

Dep<u>art</u>ment store

G<u>ar</u>dens

Superm<u>ar</u>ket

Coffee b<u>ar</u>

Ph<u>ar</u>macy

C<u>ar</u> p<u>ar</u>k

2 Look and learn

b)

| supermarket | car park | pharmacy | gardens |

d) The word 'arm' is inside the word 'pharmacy'.

The word 'part' is inside the word 'department'.

Page 52

Practise the spelling

1 How far is the supermarket?   100 metres

How far is the garden centre?   2 kilometres

How far is the children's play park?   100 metres

How far is the car park?   500 metres

How far is the snack bar?   Round the corner

How far is the farmer's market?   100 metres

2

	1 M	A	R	C	H			
				2 A	R	M		
		3 C	A	R	D			
				4 P	A	R	T	Y
5 L	A	R	G	E				
				6 S	T	A	R	T

Unit 14 A holiday

Page 54

Think about the meaning

1 What will Carmen and Luis want to do? Walk in the countryside/walk through the woods/walk along the river bank.

What will Jose want to do? Play football, tennis, etc.

What will Ana want to do? Play in the play park/visit the zoo/play on the bouncy castle/play in the ball pit.

What will Carmen's mother want to do? Relax in the flower garden.

Page 55

1 Find the words

Come and stay at Riverside Holiday Park

The park is set in beautiful countryside. Take a walk through the woods or along the river bank to the waterfall. Or relax in our lovely flower gardens.

We have a large sports hall, for badminton, table tennis and basketball. We also have a well-equipped gym, tennis courts and a football pitch.

For younger children, there is always lots to do. We have toys, play parks, with bouncy castle and ball pit, and lots of fun activities.

We even have a small animal zoo.

With comfortable rooms, good restaurants, cafes and bars, Riverside Holiday Park is perfect for all the family.

For more information call **0800** --------- Or visit **www.Riverhols.com**

Think about the spelling

1 **Listen and learn**

d) hall   (sentence a)
    hole   (sentence b)
    walk   (sentence c)
    woke   (sentence d)
    hole   (sentence b)
    walk   (sentence c)
    woke   (sentence d)
    hall   (sentence a)

Page 56

Practise the spelling

1

A round object – there are many games you can play with it	ball
The opposite of 'big'	small
Every building needs four or more of these	wall
Speak to someone on the phone	call

2 a) Basketball players are usually very tall.

b) Call me if you have any problems.

c) There are three new courts in the badminton hall.

d) In a game of squash, you hit the ball against a wall.

e) Look after small children in the play park. Make sure they don't fall.

f) When you finish playing football, you can buy food and drink at the refreshment stall.

3 a) He loves football, but he also plays cricket and tennis.

b) We expected him to arrive at 3 o'clock, but it's only 2 o'clock, and he's here already.

c) She always arrives early or on time, never late.

Unit 15 Supermarket shopping

Page 58

Think about the meaning

What are the special offers on?

- Meat? 350 grams minced beef for the price of 250.
- Fresh vegetables? Two packets of green beans for the price of one.
  Mixed leaf salad – buy one get one free.
- Frozen foods?
  Free chocolate bar with two tubs of chocolate ice cream.
  Free frozen mixed vegetables with 1kg packet of frozen peas.
- Other items? 20% off French cheeses.
  Only 15p for a 125 gram tin of baked beans.
  Tea bags – 3 for the price of 2.

Page 59

Think about the spelling

1 **Find the words** and **2** **Look and learn** a)

Words with 'ee'	Words with 'ea'
green	beans
week	tea
free	cream
beef	lean
cheeses	leaf
sleep	peas
see	cheap (cheaper)
street	clean
feel	eat
	meal
	please

3 Listen and learn

c) bin

bean

sheep

ship

bin

ship

bean

sheep

Page 60

Practise the spelling

1 "There's a new café in the main <u>street</u>. It's very good".

"Is it expensive?"

"No, it's very <u>cheap</u>."

"What can you get there?"

"A cup of tea or coffee, coca cola, lemonade. You can get a full cooked meal or you can have sandwiches. They have chicken sandwiches, but if you don't eat meat, there are cheese.or egg sandwiches"

2

green	clean
street	eat
sleep	cheap
see	tea
feel	meal
cheese	please

Page 61

Learn how to learn

1   This dictionary has the words but not the meaning.
    Spelling dictionary

2   This dictionary is good for anyone who speaks English.
    Complete English–English dictionary

3   This dictionary has words in two languages.
    Bilingual dictionary

4   This dictionary is a kind of handheld computer.
    Electronic dictionary

5   This dictionary does not have very difficult words.
    Learner's English–English dictionary

Unit 16 The library

Page 62

Think about the meaning

a) What are the opening times of the library? 9am to 5pm.

b) What do you do if you want to watch a DVD? Book a time in the audio visual room.

c) If the book you want is not in the library, what can you do? Order it.

d) What is the rule about food and drink? Do not bring food and drink.

e) What is the rule about mobile phones? Switch them off.

Page 63

Think about the spelling

1 Find the words

AUDIO-VISUAL <u>ROOM</u>

Please <u>book</u> a time if you

want to use a computer or

watch a DVD

Are you <u>looking</u> for a <u>good</u> <u>book</u> to read?

Come and <u>look</u> in the <u>school</u> library

<u>Choose</u> any <u>book</u> you like

We have <u>books</u> on all subjects from computer

science to <u>cookery</u> and are open from

9am to 5pm every day

**Do not bring <u>food</u>
and drink into the
library**

Switch **OFF** mobile phones

If the <u>book</u> you want is not in the
library, you can order it.
Tell us and we will contact you as
<u>soon</u> as it comes in.

Page 64

Practise the spelling

1 a) Has anyone got any food? I'm really hungry.

b) Let's go to the zoo to see the animals.

c) He hurt his foot in a running accident.

d) That's a really good idea.

e) I like both of them. It's difficult to choose one.

f) I left school when I was 14.

g) My sister works in a canteen. She's a cook.

2

rude	food
fruit	boot
blue	zoo
shoes	choose
rule	school

3 The sky is blue

Let's go to the zoo

Page 65

Learn how to learn

1

actor	cinema	daughter	eggs	fish	glass
hotel	jeans	kitchen	newspaper	quiz	shop
town	van	yesterday			

2

sell	September	solicitor	sometimes	son	spelling
station	stop	street	Sunday		

3

daughter	education	tomorrow	independent

Unit 17 The local council

Page 66

Think about the meaning

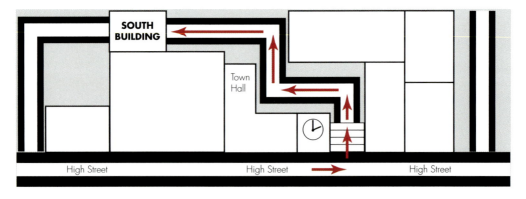

Page 67

Think about the spelling

1 Find the words

Your local <u>councillors</u> are:

Janet Greenwood, Mohammed Akram and James Moon

We are available to talk to you <u>about</u> the things that concern you, such as:

- Education
- <u>Housing</u>
- Safety in the community

Come along to
the <u>South</u> Building of the <u>Council</u> Offices
any
Tuesday or Friday, 6 – 8 p.m.

<u>How</u> to find us

Find the old <u>Town</u> Hall in the High Street. Take the path to the right of the Clock <u>Tower</u> on the <u>outside</u> of the building, then go <u>down</u> the steps and <u>round</u> the corner of the main building. You will see the <u>South</u> Building in front of you.

---

2 Look and learn

a) and b)

Words with 'ow'	Words with 'ou'
how	councillors
down	south
town	round
tower	outside
brown	council
towel	about
now	housing
flower	mouse
	found
	pound
	loud
	house
	sound

3 a) You drop the 'e' in 'house' when you add 'ing' (like the examples in Unit 12).

4 Listen and learn

b) i) 'Flour' is used for cooking.

ii) A 'flower is something you see in a park or garden.

Page 68

Practise the spelling

1 a) I found a pound coin in the street.

b) There's a nice flower shop in the centre of town.

c) They are living in their new house now.

d) I can't use the computer. I need to buy a new mouse.

e) Can you turn the radio down? It's too loud for me.

f) I'm going swimming. Where can I find a clean towel?

g) All the words in the gaps have the same vowel sound.

2

¹P	O	U	²N	D		³C	O	W	⁴S
U			O			A			O
⁵L	O	U	D		⁶B	R	O	⁷W	N
L								I	
	⁸M	O	U	N	T	A	I	N	
	O							⁹U	
¹⁰M	O	U	¹¹T	H		¹²T	O	W	N
A			I			W			I
¹³D	O	W	N		¹⁴C	O	U	N	T

Unit 18 Train travel

Page 70

a) What time does the 16.38 train from Leeds arrive in Hull?
    17.37

b) If you want to go somewhere for one day, what type of ticket can you buy?
    Same day return.

c) If you buy an 'advance' ticket, can you travel on any train you like?
    No, it must be on the date and at the time on your ticket.

d) Where can you buy a railcard?
    Online, by telephone or in person at a mainline station.

e) Is a railcard free?
    No, it costs £28.

Page 71

1 **Find the words**

a), b) and c)

YOUR Train Travel

HOME   SERVICES   ABOUT   CONTACT

Find train times

From Leeds to Hull leaving today at 16.30

Depart	From	To	Arrive	Duration	Changes
16.38	Leeds	Hull	17.37	59 m.	0
17.38	Leeds	Hull	18.40	1 h. 02 m.	0

Find earlier trains   Find later trains

TICKET TYPES

Advance tickets
Advance tickets are single (one-way) tickets. You must book in advance, and tickets are cheaper if you book early. **Please note**: advance tickets are not available on all trains, and you must travel on the date and at the time on your ticket.

OFF-PEAK TICKETS

Off-peak tickets are cheaper tickets for times when trains are not busy
Same day return
You must make your outward and return journeys on the same day. **Please note**: These tickets are normally only valid after 9.30 a.m. and your ticket may not be valid on **all** trains after this time.

RAILCARDS

You can save one third of the ticket price on most rail journeys if you have a railcard, for example: Family and Friends, 16–25, Senior, Disabled Person's Railcard. For more information, **click here**

You can buy your railcard on-line, by telephone or in person at any mainline station. You pay £28 for the card, and it is valid for one year.

2 **Look and learn**

After 'ai' there is a consonant, but after 'ay' there isn't.

3 **Listen and learn**

c)

1)	He had a pen in his hand	(i)
2)	He had a pain in his hand	(ii)
3)	He had a pain in his hand	(ii)
4)	He had a pen in his hand	(i)
5)	He had a pen in his hand	(i)
6)	He had a pain in his hand	(ii)

Page 72

Practise the spelling

1 a) Water that falls from the sky.   Rain

    b) The part of your body that controls everything.   Brain

    c) A way of writing to a person on a computer.   Email

    d) A man who serves food in a restaurant.   Waiter

    e) Something you put on your walls with a brush to change the colour.   Paint

    f) A European country near Portugal and France.   Spain

2 Some possible words: gay, hay, lay, may, pay, ray, say, way
Some possible words: pray, play, tray

3 Can you give me some information about trains to Birmingham today?

Are you coming back today?

Yes, what's the cheapest way to travel?

A cheap day return is best, but you have to wait until 10.15. That's the first train after 9.30.

That's fine.

Do you have a railcard?

No. How do I get one?

Are you aged between 16 and 25?

Yes, I'm 22.

Then you fill in this form and pay for the railcard. After that you save money on your journey today and all the off-peak journeys you make this year.
How much is it?

Unit 19 Sightseeing

Page 74

a) Did Rani fly in the daytime?
No, it was a night flight.

b) Who came to meet her at the airport?
Nearly all the family.

c) What was the weather like on Friday afternoon?
Good, with bright sunshine.

d) Where did they go on Sunday?
To a small town in the mountains.

e) How did they get to the top of the mountain?
By cable car.

f) How long did they stay there?
Till after dark.

g) What could they see at the end of their time on the mountain?
The lights in the town below and in the distance.

Page 75

Think about the spelling

1 Find the words

Thursday
Arrived on time, but exhausted. The flight was good, no delays, but night flights are always tiring. Nearly all the family came to meet me at the airport – it was great – lots to talk about. They all send their love to everybody in the UK.

Friday
Spent time resting, while most of the family are at work. I sat in the garden most of the day. The weather is good – really bright sunshine this afternoon.

Monday
Yesterday we went sight-seeing. This place is beautiful! We went to a small town in the mountains, and the weather was just right – not too hot, not too cold. There's a cable car that goes up one of the mountains, straight up the side of the mountain – rocks one side, nothing the other!!! Very scary, but impressive. We were really high up, with a fantastic view all around. The best thing was that we stayed there till after dark, and it was fascinating to see all the lights come on in the town below and in the distance too.

Going shopping now – will try not to spend too much.

2 Look and learn

b)

't' normally comes after 'igh'.

The word that does not have this letter is 'high'.

Page 76

Practise the spelling

1 a) Go straight ahead for about 100 metres, then turn left and take the first turning on the right.

b) Is it OK if I turn the light on? It's very dark in here.

c) I'm working the day shift this week, but next week I'm on the night shift.

d) Welcome to flight number 2987 to New York. This is your captain speaking.

e) There was a big fight between two gangs in the street. We had to call the police.

f) Does the jacket fit you well?
No, it's too tight. I need a bigger size.

g) Would you like another cake?
No, thanks, I'm trying to lose weight.

2 a) right / write

Can you write it down for me?

First turn left, then turn right.

I write with my right hand.

b) sight / site

It was a beautiful sight.

He works on a building site.

c) higher/ hire

I don't want to buy the tools for the job. I want to hire them.

These mountains are higher than the mountains in my country.

Unit 20 Road signs

Page 78

Think about the meaning

1

Go slow   Low bridge ahead   Shallow water   Narrow road
Road works
ahead

2 a) Fast – Slow

b) Wide – Narrow

c) High – Low

d) Deep – Shallow

Page 79

Think about the spelling

1 **Find the words**

1    2   3    4

5    6   7

2 **Look and learn**

a) You normally write 'oa' in the middle of a word, and 'ow' at the end of a word.

b)

goal	coat	toast	boat	soap	road

c)

Words with 'oa'	Words with 'ow'	Words with 'o'
road	low	go
boat	show	so
soap	slow	no
coat	snow	
goal	grow	
toast	know	

Page 80

Practise the spelling

1

2 *Know or no?*

Is it cold outside? No, it isn't.
Is it cold outside? I don't know.

Knows or nose?

My nose is cold.
He knows it's cold.

Unit 21 A personal account

Page 82

	Jane	Diana's husband	Emma
Where they live – the city – the area	Leeds Near the city centre	Bristol Near the countryside	London In an industrial area
Where they work	At home	In a library	In a computer company

Page 83

Think about the spelling

1 **Find the words**

a) and b)

My name is Jane and I live with my family. I am married with two teenage children and one baby! Before my baby was born, I worked part time in an office, but now I work for the same company from my own home. I have a photocopier, fax machine and of course the Internet, so I can keep in touch with my boss. She sends emails and faxes for me to deal with, so I don't need to go to the office much. I go to a computer class once a week. There is a day nursery at the college, so my baby goes there. Last year I also went to English classes for two days a week, but not this year.

My husband works in an electrical goods factory. He has a very long journey to work, so he leaves early and comes back late. Luckily, his company is moving to the city centre. This is good, because we live near the city centre. As for me, I have no journeys to work!

I have two sisters, Diana and Emma, but they don't live near me. In fact, the three of us all live in different cities: me in Leeds, Diana in Bristol and Emma in London. My sister Diana lives near the countryside, but Emma lives in an industrial area. There are a lot of factories near where she lives.

Both my sisters are married. Emma and her husband work for computer companies, but not the same one. Diana's husband has a job in a library. Diana works two days a week as a childminder. She looks after two babies, but she's also studying part-time to be a nursery teacher. There are some good nurseries where she lives. There is also a large family centre, where they look after children for working families, so I think there are good job opportunities for Diana.

2 **Look and learn**

a)

Singular	Plural
family	families
city	cities
nursery	nurseries
factory	factories
company	companies
baby	babies
journey	journeys
day	days

'Journey' and 'day' are different because they don't change 'y' to 'i'. They only add 's'. Both words have another vowel before the 'y'. Words with another vowel before 'y' do not change the 'y' to 'ies'.

c) books   tables   chairs   cakes   bananas   cups   dogs   biscuits
    lights   faxes   classes

'Faxes' and 'classes' add an 'e' before the 's'. The regular plurals only add 's'. 'Fax' and 'class' end in a 's' sound, so they need an 'e' before the plural 's'.

Page 84

Practise the spelling

1 a) Key   Keys

   b) Library   Libraries

   c) Cross   Crosses

   d) Box   Boxes

   e) Lady   Ladies

   f) Boy   Boys

   g) Tax   Taxes

   h) Dress   Dresses

   i) Copy   Copies

2 a) Put the books in the bags.

   b) Put the dresses in the boxes.

   c) Who are the ladies over there?

   d) We saw two football matches.

   e) Can I make some photocopies?

   f) They have two babies.

   g) We bought some watches.

   h) We went to the zoo and saw some monkeys.

Page 85

Learn how to learn

Learn common endings

1 Photocopier

   Computer

   Sister

   Childminder

   Teacher

2 Read the text for Unit 19 'Sightseeing' and find one word ending in ' ...ive'.
Impressive

Read the text for Unit 12 'Driving lessons' and find another word ending in '..ive'.
Intensive

Read the text for Unit 14 'A holiday' and find one word ending in '...able'.
Comfortable

Read the text for Unit 15 'Supermarket shopping' and find another word ending in '...able'.
Vegetable

Read the text for Unit 13 'In the town' and find one word ending in '...tion'.
Station

Read the text for Unit 17 'The Local Council' and find another word ending in '...tion'.
Education

Unit 22 A traditional story

Page 86

Think about the meaning

1) The man and boy walked with the donkey   (b)

2) The man sat on the donkey   (a)

3) The boy sat on the donkey   (e)

4) The man and boy both sat on the donkey   (c)

5) The man and boy carried the donkey   (d)

6) The man and boy walked with the donkey (again)   (b)

The moral of the story is that if you try to please everybody, you please nobody.

Page 87

Think about the spelling

1 **Find the words**

a)

Base form	Past tense		Base form	Past tense
walk	walked		stop	stopped
laugh	laughed		grab	grabbed
want	wanted		cry	cried
start	started		carry	carried
shout	shouted		hurry	hurried
climb	climbed		try	tried

b) 'Stop' and 'grab' double the last consonant.
'Cry', 'carry', 'hurry' and 'try' change 'y' to 'ied'.

2 Look and learn

b)

Add 'ed'	Double consonant + 'ed'	Change 'y' to 'i' + 'ed'
wanted	stopped	carried
started	planned	copied
finished	jogged	fried
talked	fitted	married

3 Listen and learn

'Walked', 'laughed' and 'stopped' have a 't' sound at the end.
You hear the vowel sound in 'wanted', 'started' and 'shouted'.

Page 88

Practise the spelling

1 They started to walk along the path towards the market.

Some people stopped them.

The man wanted to please the people.

The man and the boy grabbed the donkey, lifted it and carried it down the road towards the market.

The next people laughed until they cried.

So the man and the boy put the donkey down, walked beside the donkey, and with their heads down, they hurried to the market.

2 a) I stopped the car at the traffic lights.

b) I carried my books in my bag.

c) They jogged in the park in the morning.

d) We always photocopied our work.

e) When they cooked, they always fried the potatoes.

f) I always tried to help them.

3 a) My sister is getting married next month.

b) I want fresh tomatoes, not tinned tomatoes.

c) I would like to have a fitted carpet in my room.